# UNDERSTANDING DISABILITY

## From Theory to Practice

**Michael Oliver**
*Professor of Disability Studies*
*The University of Greenwich*

palgrave

Published by
PALGRAVE
Houndmills, Basingstoke, Hampshire RG21 6XS and
175 Fifth Avenue, New York, N.Y. 10010
Companies and representatives throughout the world

PALGRAVE is the new global academic imprint of
St. Martin's Press LLC Scholarly and Reference Division and
Palgrave Publishers Ltd (formerly Macmillan Press Ltd).

ISBN 0–333–59915–2 hardback
ISBN 0-312-015803-3 paperback

This book is printed on paper suitable for recycling and
made from fully managed and sustained forest sources.

A catalogue record for this book is available
from the British Library.

8    7
02

# ONE WEEK LOAN

*Also by Michael Oliver*

SOCIAL WORK WITH DISABLED PEOPLE*

WALKING INTO DARKNESS: The Experience of Spinal Cord Injury (*with M. Moore, V. Salisbury, J. Silver and G. Zarb*)*

THE POLITICS OF DISABLEMENT*

SOCIAL WORK: Disabled People and Disabling Environments (*editor*)

AGEING WITH A DISABILITY: What do They Expect After All These Years? (*with G. Zarb*)

DISABLING BARRIERS – ENABLING ENVIRONMENTS (*edited with J. Swain, V. Finkelstein and S. French*)

\* from the same publishers

*To Joy Melinda Oliver*
*and Georgina Ryall*

It's coming through a hole in the air,
from those nights in Tiananmen Square.
It's coming from the feel
that it ain't exactly real,
or it's real but it ain't exactly there.
From the wars against disorder,
from the sirens night and day,
from the fires of the homeless,
from the ashes of the gay:
Democracy is coming . . .

# Contents

# List of Tables

# Acknowledgements

In the course of my life, I have been influenced by so many people that it is impossible to credit them all. My dilemma is that once I start to name people who have influenced what I have written here, where do I stop and who might I leave out or inadvertently forget? In deciding to name no one I may appear to be ungrateful to people who have shared their time, experience and ideas with me but I am indebted to them all.

Despite my word processor, I would still have been incapable of providing this manuscript unaided and so I thank Cathy Lewington for keeping me sane and allowing me to focus on the ideas and issues contained herein.

Finally, I am grateful to Vic Finkelstein for allowing me to use material from the Fundamental Principles document and to Lois Keith for permission to print her poem in full.

MICHAEL OLIVER

# Introduction

It was nearly twenty years ago that I began writing about disability issues and since then I have published widely in books, academic journals, magazines, newspapers and disability journals. The original idea for this book was that, because much of this writing was in books or journals not easily available, a collection of my papers put into one place would be useful.

When I came to plan the book in more detail, my initial idea was that I would organise it as a chronology, showing how my own thinking and understanding had developed historically. When I then went back and re-read some of this old work, I was immediately struck by two things; firstly, I found that my thinking had changed very little. The initial simple idea from which I began, namely that disability was the product of social organisation rather than personal limitation, had remained unaltered. What had happened was that, over the years, I had used this simple idea and applied it to a number of different contexts or issues. Thus, although my thinking about disability in general had changed little, my understanding of particular issues had grown enormously.

I should say at this point that the original simple idea underpinning my work was not my original idea but was an idea that

1

I came across in encountering *Fundamental Principles of Disability* (UPIAS 1976) for the first time. This slim volume is not widely available but the debt that disabled people owe to it is enormous. It is for this reason that I have included an edited version as Chapter 2. Even today, it states more clearly than I could what I think about disability.

This led to the second thing that struck me about my own work. While it remained true to the idea that underpinned it, the application of that idea to particular issues and contexts seemed outdated both in terms of the language used and because the world had moved on; new legislation, new organisations, new methods of action and so on. Given this situation, I quickly realised that simply publishing my past work would be of limited use or interest to other people.

As well as these problems, I was also aware that much of this previous work had been criticised, particularly by other disabled people and that in any new publication I ought to try to respond to these criticisms. The first major criticism was that much of my writing was inaccessible to many disabled people because it was too academic. The second main criticism, particularly from disabled women, was that there was a personal or subjective dimension lacking in what I had written.

While the inaccessibility of my writing has been eloquently defended by others, notably Hevey, who suggests that

> Although *The Politics of Disablement* does mobilise difficult language in its arguments, Mike Oliver can hardly be blamed, as some people have been attempting to blame him, for 'inaccessible theory' *per se*. It is, after all, not his fault that psychoanalysis, marxism and discourse theory are not taught within segregated education! The question is, of course, do the theoretical tools which Mike Oliver uses have a benefit and purpose within the disability movement?
>
> (Hevey 1991)

The issue of the value of theory will be returned to at later stages in the book.

My own response to the criticism that my work is too academic is somewhat different. While it may be true that I do not always communicate my ideas as clearly as I might, understanding disability requires a great deal of intellectual effort. If we are going to transform ourselves and society, it is only we as disabled people who can do the necessary intellectual work. Therefore, in this volume, while I will try to communicate with clarity, I refuse to oversimplify the complexity of the ideas and issues which produce disability in the late twentieth century.

This is not a view that all disabled people will accept and they will argue that it will serve to exclude some disabled people from both their personal and political journeys towards understanding themselves, their material circumstances and their social situations. At times this view borders on anti-intellectualism and it is for this reason that the final chapter is, in part, a discussion of the role of intellectuals in the disability movement.

As far as the absence of a personal or subjective dimension to my writing is concerned, there are two reasons for this. There is a thin line between writing subjectively and exposing things which are and should remain private. There is no doubt that women are much better and more practised at treading this line. That doesn't mean that as men, we should not attempt to tread it and Chapter 1 is an attempt to do this and hence provide a subjective framework for the rest of the book.

There is another issue at stake here, however, which is discussed more fully in Chapter 3. There is a danger in emphasising the personal at the expense of the political because most of the world still thinks of disability as an individual, intensely personal problem. And many of those who once made a good living espousing this view would be only too glad to come out of the woodwork and say that they were right all along.

Returning to my own subjective framework, Chapters 4, 5 and 6 are concerned with issues of social and educational policy which are personal to me in two senses. Personal because I, like all disabled people, come into contact with the services provided under these policies and need to make sense of the profound difference between the rhetoric of policy and the reality of provision. Personal also, in that as an academic, I spend much of my professional life teaching about these issues and also undertaking research and consultancy work in order to influence their future directions.

Chapter 7 is about an issue even more intensely personal to me; that of walking, or rather not walking. As well as having an obvious personal interest in the topic, the first paper I ever published as a junior academic was on the topic and I returned to it as the theme for my inaugural professorial lecture in 1992.

It is this latter paper which forms the basis for the chapter. Those of you expecting that the chapter will explore my own feelings about not walking will be disappointed however; it is much more an exploration of the ways in which our culture and our rehabilitation services produce and sustain a particular view of the world.

The next chapter is a first attempt to fill a gap in my own knowledge about disability – what we know, or rather what we don't know about international aspects of disability. Despite the existence of an international disability movement, we know little about the experience of disability world wide, there is almost no global theorising about disability, few comparative studies worth the paper they were written on and little or no research which is not solely reliant on the medical model or the WHO classification scheme (Wood 1980). It would be absurd to suggest that Chapter 8 can be anything other than a memo to me, and hopefully other disabled people, that this is an area where much work needs to be done.

Chapter 9 integrates aspects of the personal in that it is an attempt to pull together some of my own theorising as a sociologist with research that I have undertaken over the years. Central to this is the experience of growing old with disability which seems to become even more intensely personal to me as every year passes. It also owes a considerable debt to Gerry Zarb with whom I have worked over many years and it is impossible to disentangle where my ideas stopped and his began and vice versa.

This is also true of all the other ideas contained herein. I make no claim that any of them are original and even if they are, I have even more trouble with the concept of private intellectual property than I do other kinds of property. Throughout the book I attempt to acknowledge the ideas and influence of other disabled people, sociologists, cultural icons and the like, but the final product is mine and I take responsibility for it.

The final two chapters return to the theme of the personal and the political and seek both to update my own thinking about the disability movement as a new social movement and the role of individuals within such movements. It is an attempt to further my own understanding of the political potential of the disability movement and my own role within it. If it also helps others in their understandings, then this is important because as others have argued, and I shall argue, understanding ourselves is a key element in transforming our world.

In order to help those who are either interested in seeing how my thinking has developed or in furthering their own understandings of disability issues, each of the following chapters will begin with an introduction which describes when and why the chapters were first written and how they have subsequently been developed for inclusion here. Accordingly, the book can be seen as an intellectual journey and be read as such; starting from the beginning and reading right through. Alternatively, each chapter is about a specific topic and so the book can be dipped into.

There is a final point I need to make here and this concerns the issue of language. Throughout I shall attempt to remain within the distinction between impairment and disability developed by UPIAS and reproduced in Chapter 2. Following on from this, my definition of disabled people contains three elements; (i) the presence of an impairment; (ii) the experience of externally imposed restrictions; and (iii) self-identification as a disabled person. This book therefore is about disabled people, not people with impairments and should be read as such.

In what follows I shall attempt to use this linguistic framework consistently but this in itself is a struggle and errors can creep in. In addition, what is acceptable can change over time, even between writing something and the text appearing in published form. For instance, when I wrote *The Politics of Disablement* there was a debate going on about the terms learning difficulty and mental handicap. By the time the book came out the debate had been resolved and I had chosen wrongly. In Chapter 6 of this volume there is a similar and yet-to-be-resolved debate about integration/segregation or inclusion/exclusion. The point is that language is a process whereas a book is a product and there are bound to be examples of 'politically incorrect' usage, if only because of changes over time.

One of the things that has become apparent to me over the years, is that the link between personal experience and what people write cannot be ignored and should not be denied. This is not to say that all writing is autobiographical nor that one can only write about those things that have been experienced personally. However personal experience does have a direct, if complex, influence both on what gets written and the way it gets written. It is this link between my own personal experience and what I have written that I explore in the next chapter.

# 1
# From Personal Struggle to Political Understanding

## Introduction

This opening chapter will be an attempt for me to understand retrospectively the development of my own personal and political consciousness. Unlike later chapters, this has been specially written for this book, though earlier versions of my own thinking about role models and my professional career have appeared elsewhere. It is rooted in my own personal biography which I briefly outline. A more detailed description of my life may appear as an autobiography once I retire or, if my pension proves inadequate, as a thinly disguised novel.

This reflexive account will focus on three areas which, for analytical purposes, I will separate into (1) looking at my growing political awareness, (2) the way my career developed and the influence this had on my growing political consciousness, and (3) my growing involvement with disabled people and the organisations which we were creating and the effect that this had on my developing understanding of disability as a personal, social and sociological phenomenon. Of course, this whole process was and is far more chaotic and confusing than any retrospective account will make it appear.

## The personal is the personal

My own personal experience of disability began in 1962. I was the only son of working class parents and had recently left the local grammar school as a failure, having only gained three O levels. Stuck in a dead end clerical job, my life centred around the cricket and football I played for local teams and the macho activities I and my mates used to often pretend, and occasionally, got up to. When I was seventeen five of us decided to go on holiday together, to a well-known holiday camp in Essex (the present-day equivalent of the package tour to Spain or Greece).

Behaving like latter-day lager louts, it was not long before I got up to something which was to transform my life. I dived into the holiday camp swimming pool, hit my head on the bottom, broke my neck and spent the next year at the world famous Stoke Mandeville Hospital. As I have written elsewhere (Oliver 1982), this was not a wholly negative experience although, of course, things like having a metal frame screwed into my skull while fully conscious, are not experiences I would want to repeat.

However, the positive far outweighed the negative. The culture of Stoke Mandeville was definitely macho, and I was encouraged to undertake as much physical activity as I wanted. Additionally, there were the women; nurses, physios, OTs, all of whom were in close proximity and many of whom were required to perform professional acts of intimacy. It is not surprising that the boundaries between these professional and personal acts of intimacy were often blurred in the evenings and at weekends, given that the majority of the patients were young men and the majority of the staff were young women.

I think I learned more about myself and personal relationships in the one year I spent there than I have subsequently in the twenty years I spent in another kind of institution, the university. But there were other important gains as well. My relationships with my parents and other family members grew stronger at a time when often for young people such relationships grow weaker as they strive for independence. On leaving hospital, my mates and the working class community which I had left welcomed me back.

For a while, all was well. My life continued as it had before the accident except that I did not have a boring clerical job to go to. Soon it became apparent that endless days without boring work were even more boring than endless days with it and while my family remained close and supportive, I began to feel restless and that there must be more to life than watching television, being taken out by your mates and drinking. The next major change in my life occurred not because of the successful intervention of skilled professionals but purely by luck.

## The personal and the professional

My professional interest in disability did not really come about until some ten years after I became disabled as the result of the spinal injury in 1962. After my year in Stoke Mandeville Hospital, I spent three years unemployed and thinking I was unemployable – a perception that was reinforced by every single professional I met during that time. In 1966, purely by chance, I was offered a job as a clerk at the young offenders' prison near where I lived.

Despite my previous boring experience as a clerk I was persuaded by the charismatic principal of the education centre in the prison that this was a great opportunity. I did not need much persuading and within a matter of months the not-so-boring clerical job had changed and I became a lecturer in the education centre of the same establishment and remained there for six years. However, being unqualified, in 1972 I went to university and read for a degree in sociology. On completion, I remained for a further three years to undertake research and gain my doctorate.

As a postgraduate student, my interests were in the fields of deviance and crime rather than illness and disability. The positivist view dominated the academic world at this time; according to this, one did not become involved in subjects in which one had a personal involvement or interest because this made objectivity very difficult, if not impossible.

However, as a postgraduate student with a young family to support, one of the few occasions when disability became a positive advantage was when the Open University began looking for course tutors for its new disability course. In addition in my own research I was exploring the supposed links between crime and epilepsy (Oliver 1979, 1980) and this inevitably meant that I had to read some medical sociology because epilepsy was conceptualised as illness rather than deviance. I quickly discovered that then, as now, many medical sociologists proceed on the assumption that illness and disability are the same thing.

When I began to read some of the things that able-bodied academics, researchers and professionals had written about disability, I was staggered at how little it related to my own experience of disability or indeed, of most other disabled people I had come to know. Over the next few years it gradually began to dawn on me that if disabled people left it to others to write about disability, we would inevitably end up with inaccurate and distorted accounts of our experiences and inappropriate service provision and professional practices based upon these inaccuracies and distortions.

Incidentally, it was at this point in history that women were beginning to reject male accounts of their experiences and black people were vehemently denying the accuracy of white descriptions of what it was like to be black. This questioning had reverberations throughout the academic world, calling into question the whole notion of objectivity and bringing subjectivity onto the academic agenda.

As a sociologist I found myself supporting the call for a committed and partisan sociology (Gouldner 1975). As a disabled person I found myself empathising with the position of feminists who saw ' . . . objectivity as the word men use to talk about their own subjectivity' (Rich, quoted in Morris 1992). As a disabled sociologist I found myself in the 'academic disability ghetto' but determined to render an accurate, undistorted and wholly subjective account of disability.

I have no regrets about being in the disability ghetto. It has enabled me to teach about disability issues to students at the Universities of Kent and Greenwich where I have worked as a full-time academic, as well as at a whole range of other assorted universities, polytechnics and colleges. As well as undergraduate and postgraduate students, I have been involved in both initial and post-qualifying training to professional groups including social workers, teachers, nurses, occupational therapists and physiotherapists and so on.

Before leaving this academic part of my biography, I need

to return to my involvement with the Open University. In particular, its first course on disability issues 'The Handicapped
Person in the Community' had a key influence on my thinking. While it was based upon the assumptions that disability
was a condition of the individual and that the way to deal with
it was through professional interventions designed to deal with
either the medical complications or functional limitations of
impaired individuals, it nonetheless provided both an opportunity to read some of the academic literature on disability
and an academic focus to take further my thinking on disability.

In addition this involvement gave me the opportunity to work
with Vic Finkelstein. While I knew Vic, and that he had had a
key influence on the 'Fundamental Principles' document, it
was not until then that I realised the importance of the work
we were beginning to undertake in re-defining disability.

By the time the 'Handicapped Person' course came to be
re-written, we had both written major critiques of the individual
model of disability, as it came to be called (Finkelstein 1980,
Oliver 1983). These critiques had called into question the ap-
propriateness of professional interventions based upon this model
and the re-written course was much more centrally concerned
to create a partnership with professionals.

The world has now moved on and the production of a completely new course entitled 'The Disabling Society' reflects further changes in our understandings of the nature of disability.
By now disability has been redefined by many disabled people
and their representative organisations as the social barriers,
restrictions and/or oppressions they face and professional interventions have come to be seen as often adding to these problems rather than seeking to deal with them.

These changes are, therefore, a part of my own personal
biography for, in one way or another, I have been involved in
these courses almost since the beginning, initially as a course
tutor and then as a member of the course teams for the re-
write and production of the new course. Hence it would not
be inaccurate to say that changes in my own thinking about
disability were both reflected in and influenced by changes in
the OU courses. And it should perhaps be added, that these
courses have had a profound effect on the way others have
thought about disability, among them disabled people and
professionals in particular.

## The personal becomes the political

To return to my own developing consciousness of disability issues, my original attitude was one which is not uncommon today. It can perhaps be best characterised by the term 'denial'; not denial as it is usually seen by professionals, that is, as a pathological response to my own impairment, but a denial of the fact that I might have anything in common with other disabled people. So I actively sought to avoid contact with other disabled people wherever possible, either on the street or by joining organisations.

This avoidance was only partial however, because prior to my accident I had been a keen sportsman and my interest remained. Hence for many years I participated in what were then called 'the Stoke Mandeville Games', at both national and international level. While I think the value of sport for disabled people is over-stated in therapeutic and rehabilitative terms, there is no doubt that it was valuable to me personally; it enabled me to maintain a positive self-identity, it made my denial only partial and it embedded me in a network of social relationships, many of which remain today.

It also provided me with my first experience of collective action. There was a move to exclude tetraplegics from some of the more prestigious international events because it was argued that their needs for personal assistance were too great. The real truth was that providing personal assistants to disabled people would have drastically reduced the places available for the hangers on who bedevil all sports. A few of us organised ourselves and mobilised support from other competitors and the plan was quickly dropped, publicly at least. The victory was only partial of course, because behind the scenes machinations continued to exclude some of us but the experience of political action was an empowering one even if I did not see it as political at the time.

Around this time I was also trying to acquire the educational qualifications I had missed out on as a working class failure of the grammar school system, and this was proving no easy matter. Poor access to educational buildings coupled with disablist attitudes of many educators meant that a thick skin was a necessary pre-requisite for kicking open the door of educational opportunity. I soon realised that if that door was not only to be kicked open for those individuals powerful enough to do so, but was also to remain open, individual action could never be enough.

As my undergraduate career was coming to an end, I heard of an initiative to keep this door permanently open by creating an organisation which became the National Bureau for Handicapped Students. I attended the inaugural conference and eagerly joined its council of management. At the same time, there was a move to form an impairment specific self-help group for people with spinal injuries. Again I attended the inaugural meeting, and as soon as my studies permitted, I joined the management committee of the Spinal Injuries Association.

Over the next few years, my experiences of collective action in these two groups differed radically. SIA was controlled by disabled people, it knew its mission was to represent people with a spinal injury and it was not afraid to speak out, tread on toes or offend vested interests. I was never sure who controlled NBHS but I quickly came to realise that its (unspoken) mission was to protect the interests of educational establishments and the staff who worked in them; it rarely spoke out on anything and most of the vested interests were represented on its council of management.

As a result I left NBHS in disillusion after a few years but remained with SIA for sixteen. Furthermore these experiences left me convinced that only organisations controlled by disabled people could properly represent the wishes of disabled people. My own personal experience had convinced me of something of general importance and I found support for this in the sociological literature.

> Social theories are grounded in the knowledge the theorist has gained through personal experience. Facts, rooted in personal reality, are of course utterly persuasive to the theorist. He becomes involved in, sees, experiences, such things as the French Revolution, the rise of socialism, the great Depression, and he never doubts the factuality of his experience.
>
> (Gouldner 1975, p. 70)

As Gouldner concludes, I have not since doubted the factuality of that experience. Nor indeed have I had cause to; I have not since encountered a non-representative, non-democratic organisation which properly addresses, let alone represents, the collective interests of disabled people. Thus when there was a

move to form a cross-impairment, national co-ordinating organisation of disabled people, I used whatever power and influence I had within SIA to ensure they fully backed it. The
British Council of Organisations of Disabled People duly emerged
and has gone from strength to strength; more of which will be
said in later chapters. The point for here is that, with the emergence of BCODP, my personal journey from individual denial
to the collective embracement of disabled people was complete,
though my understanding of the real nature of disability was,
perhaps only just beginning.

## The personal is the political

So far, my description of my journey towards understanding
has been rooted in events that happened in my life. There is a
more personal aspect of the journey however which is about
the transformation of my own consciousness of disability from
personal trouble to political issue. Kickstarting the transformation from the personal to the political is a problem. For me it
was resolved not by becoming active in left politics which is
the traditional way for working class children, but rather through
listening to the music of Bob Dylan. His descriptions of injustice, inequality and moral outrage in his early albums had a
far greater impact on the development of my political consciousness than did my working class background.

While this exposure led to a growing political awareness, it
was a generalised awareness only. The links to the politics of
disability were non-existent at this time; there were no disabled
role models, heroes and heroines who could link my growing
awareness of inequalities and injustice and my own growing
sense of moral outrage, to my experience as a disabled person
nor, indeed, to the experience of disabled people generally.

Of course, impaired role models existed in large numbers;
heroes and heroines as well as victims and villains; Douglas
Bader, Beethoven, Julius Caesar, Richard 111, Mr Magoo, and
many more (Rieser and Mason 1990; Barnes 1992). However,
none of these role models made sense of my own experience
as a disabled person. I felt neither heroic nor victimised, I was
neither brave nor pathetic and I certainly did not see myself
as a villain, made bitter and twisted by my impairment. But I
was beginning to realise that my experiences as a disabled person
had a political as well as a personal dimension.

But the connections between disability and politics were not easy to make. It was almost as if they were deliberately kept in different cognitive spheres. Even where there were specific links between politics and disability in the lives of individual disabled people, these links were often deliberately covered up. For example, the two most famous impaired Americans were probably Franklin Delano Roosevelt and Helen Keller. He became President but most people did not even know he had an impairment; she was known for being deaf and blind but hardly anyone knew or now knows she was a committed socialist who strongly supported the Russian Revolution and the Government which came after it, when it was far from safe to do so in America.

The links between politics and disability in these two cases raise interesting questions – a politician whose impairment is denied and a disabled person whose politics is denied. It is difficult to decide which is the most unfortunate. In Britain, on the other hand, we have disabled politicians who neither deny their impairments nor their politics. The problem is that they don't see the connection between the two and they fail to embrace their impairments as part of a politics of personal identity.

The most recent example of this is the 'Special Award for Word Blindness' that the Greater Manchester Coalition of Disabled People gave to David Blunket, Shadow Minister for Health and a blind person, on the grounds that

> since his arrival at Westminster and promotion to the Shadow Cabinet [he] has never been heard to speak those immortal words 'disabled people'.
>
> (*Coalition*, December 1993)

Two of my own heroes, Antonio Gramsci and Woodrow Wilson Guthrie, were impaired but would not have understood these impairments as part of a politics of personal identity either. One died, imprisoned in Mussolini's jails for his political views, the other died imprisoned in his own head because of Huntington's Chorea. Neither saw his disabilities as an essential part of self. Neither saw his politics influenced by the personal restrictions he experienced as a consequence of his impairment. This, I suppose, is not surprising if you're confronted with the social restrictions imposed by fascist police, racist rednecks or anti-union thugs.

In my striving to relate my personal experiences of impairment to the social restrictions of disability, there were few disabled heroes in fiction, television or film. As far as writing is concerned, where impairment or disability does feature, it is usually seen as personal tragedy (Rieser and Mason 1991). Where disabled people have written about themselves, it has all too often been within the 'how I overcame my impairment/disability' genre. Film and television provided, and continue to provide, a mass of supercripple and the emotionally stunted disabled stereotypes. In recent years however, largely due to the influence of the disability movement on film or television, a few candidates for hero-worship are beginning to emerge.

My own personal favourite is paraplegic ex-war hero Luke Martin, played by Jon Voight in the film *Coming Home*: not just because of what he did to Jane Fonda, but because his personal disillusionment with the Vietnam War and its aftermath drove him to chain himself to the gates of an army recruiting station. In him, the personal nearly becomes the political, but not quite. His protest was an individual one and thus ultimately doomed to failure. He may have saved himself but the disabling society lives on; the United States continues to fight imperialistic wars in the name of freedom and by so doing continues to create impaired people in their thousands.

While, there may be emerging a variety of role models which will enable impaired people to understand their personal experiences in political terms, there still remains the problem that the cultural discourse on disability remains structured by the tragedy principle (Hevey 1993). And even amongst disabled people, this may be worse for some than others

> Ask yourselves, when you last saw a film or television drama or soap with a lesbian or gay relationship at the centre of the story? . . . Far from pulverising you with lesbian and gay material – we are deprived of personal, political and cultural representation! . . . This cultural and informational deprivation is imposed BY A SOCIETY THAT TAKES LITTLE OR NO ACCOUNT OF THE NEEDS OF lesbians and gay men! Where have I heard something like that before?.
> (Gillespie-Sells 1993, p. 24)

There are non-disabled real life heroes who helped me to link the personal with the political. For me, Muhammad Ali was not just the greatest boxer who ever lived but also one of the most important figures of the twentieth century. He embraced black pride, confronted religious bigotry and combined this with an opposition to the most obscene war in the history of humankind at great personal and financial cost. For him it was not just a matter of the personal being the political but, equally importantly, the political being the personal. He would not fight in Vietnam because he saw it as the white race making war on others. He also knew about the importance of being called by the name he wanted and he vigorously resisted being named by others; something that is also important to disabled people.

I should say at this point that I realise that my heroes are not without flaws. Woody Guthrie's treatment of women in his life was certainly less than heroic and Muhammad Ali's embracement of a religion which has added significantly to the oppression of women throughout the world is a cause for concern. But I cannot, nor would I wish to, deny or denigrate their effects on my consciousness at various points in my life. It points to the urgent need for all of us to develop our understanding of the links between all the oppressions that confront us in our personal lives as well as develop appropriate strategies to deal with them.

Two of my other heroes, Tommie Smith and John Carlos, used personal triumphs to make political statements. Having won a gold and bronze medal at the Olympic Games in Mexico City in 1968, both men stood on the victory rostrum and raised their black gloved hands in victory salute. In so doing, both knew they were giving up the potential riches that white society would offer if they sold out. To this day both have remained true to the beliefs that underpinned this gesture and work within black communities in their struggles against racism.

It is not all heroes or leaders who remain true to their communities. Working class movements have been bedeviled by leaders who became part of the bourgeoisie; black movements have encountered similar problems, naming the black bourgeoisie as 'uncle Toms'. Disabled people have a similar word for their bourgeoisie – 'tiny Tims'. The exploits of one particular American tiny Tim, a paraplegic 'mountain climber' called Ed Wellman is used to draw links between the past and present images of disabled people.

If you had a sense of *déjà vu* when you saw Wellman being piggybacked, let me remind you of where you saw the scene before. Every Christmas you see poor little pale, crippled Tiny Tim being carried through London on his father's back. What a wonderful omen for what is in store for us in the 21st Century: the 19th Century, with disabled children depending on the charity of rich men to decide whether they will die or become *well men.* [My emphasis]

(Bolte 1992, p. 4)

Within the disability movement itself there is, quite rightly, suspicion of heroes and leadership; it can so easily lead to the cult of the personality. The issue of leadership and social movements will be returned to in the final chapter. The point to be made here is that while there may be very sound political reasons for being suspicious of individuals, if there are none, there is an absence of role models which can be crucial in connecting the personal to the political. Hopefully, as the disability movement goes from strength to strength, new generations of disabled people will not have some of the difficulties of connecting to the personal and the political because there will be appropriate disabled role models in all areas of life.

## Conclusions

The purpose of this chapter has been to combine three things in terms of my own developing consciousness; my personal biography, my attempts to theorise about disability and my growing involvement with the disability movement. The links between these three areas have already been explored by feminists who have much practice in making them explicit.

The aim of social theory in the broad sense that I intend is not so much to predict and thereby master an external reality; rather, the aim is to gain insight and understanding into, as well as a perspective on, one's own lived reality in order to affect (have an affect on) and change oneself and others who together not only share but shape and constitute that reality

(Wallach Balogh 1991, p. 31)

It is certainly true that my own theorising has made a significant contribution to my own understanding of disability, but it

can also be linked directly with attempts by me and other disabled people to re-define disability.

> In other words, social theory, coming to terms with social
> life, means defining, describing, or naming our experience,
> our historical reality for ourselves rather than living with a
> definition imposed upon us.
>
> (Wallach Balogh 1991, p. 38)

But, in order to be able to name those experiences authenti-
cally and effectively, we need the collective strength of self-
organisation around us, again as women know only too well.

> Feminists and all those committed to emancipatory theoriz-
> ing must challenge the dominant, oppressive and repressive
> cultures of these institutions by creating a space and cul-
> ture, a holding environment, in which we can come to terms
> with our social realities and their representations. The on-
> going process of creating a holding environment for our-
> selves and each other, a social, intellectual space for political,
> intellectual sociability, for reflecting on our given 'realities',
> strengthens and empowers us to address and challenge the
> oppressive and repressive nature of those realities and the
> representations of those realities.
>
> (Wallach Balogh 1991, p. 41)

Hopefully the rest of this book will be a challenge to the
repressive nature of the reality of disability and its representations, especially where these realities and representations are
created by others for us.

# 2
# Fundamental Principles of Disability

## Introduction

The purpose of giving this chapter a similar title to the Fundamental Principles document is because it is deliberately derivative of it. I, and many other disabled people, openly acknowledge our debt to the document in the way it shaped our own understanding of disability. The document has never been widely available and with the demise of the Union in 1991, it will become increasingly difficult to obtain.

Its inclusion here is not merely for the historical record however. The issues it raises about definitions of disability, the role of experts, the place of experience and the nature of the political process are all timeless as far as our understanding of disability is concerned. They are not issues that have been resolved and the arguments around each are, and will remain, heated.

The document emerged out of attempts by disabled people to build their own organisations. By the early 1970s, two organisations had been formed, both stemming from letters written to the *Guardian* newspaper. The first of these was the Disablement Income Group (DIG) whose central purpose was to persuade Government to provide a national disability income to all disabled people as of right. The Union of the Physically Impaired Against Segregation was formed a little later and emerged partly out of the anti-democratic tendencies that were becoming apparent in DIG and partly to represent the views of those disabled people struggling to escape from residential care.

By the early 1970s it was apparent that the Government was not going to respond to the limited pressure exerted by DIG, and many of the 'big battalions' of the disability world (the old, established organisations for the disabled) decided to jump on the national disability income bandwagon. As a consequence, the Disability Alliance was formed. Because of the nature of its member organisations, it was even less democratic than DIG and by this time, more and more disabled people were beginning to realise that a national disability income was too limited a goal.

While UPIAS was, and remained, a relatively small organisation of disabled people, it did seek to raise these concerns onto the political agenda. This, of course, resulted in conflict and in order to try to prevent this from getting out of hand, a meeting between UPIAS and the Disability Alliance was organised. It was from this meeting that the Fundamental Principles document emerged.

In the edited version which follows, I have not tried to discuss both sides of the argument presented in the Fundamental Principles document but to provide a clear articulation of UPIAS's position. There are other academics who may wish to provide a more balanced account or to clarify the position of the Disability Alliance and there are certainly many so-called experts who continue to speak for disabled people with no awareness of the oppressive nature of such actions.

Few of those who seek to speak for us or write about our lives take seriously the need to represent our views, our lives and our struggles accurately and thus, I see no reason to seek to represent their views. This is not as negative as it sounds for in not representing such views, it is impossible to distort them. If only this were true in reverse, then it might not be necessary to write committed and explicitly partisan texts such as this one.

In order to acknowledge my own personal indebtedness to

the Fundamental Principles document, as well as to demonstrate both its historical and contemporary importance, I incorporate an edited version here. This edited version is divided
into three sections; the first is a statement of fundamental principles and the second is UPIAS's criticism of the positions
adopted both by the Disablement Income Group and the Disability Alliance in the 1970s. The third section uses the word
umbrella as a metaphor and is explained by Vic Finkelstein
who played a major role in producing the document.

> The Disability Alliance made much of its 'authority' being
> derived from an 'umbrella' organisation. I wanted to ridi-
> cule this both as a source of authority (by showing that the
> umbrella structure enabled a small number of experts to
> claim that they spoke for disabled people while at the same
> time they did not have to mix with common disabled peo-
> ple) and as a way of building a credible organisation (by
> showing that their arguments were full of holes).
>
> (Finkelstein 1994)

In the process of editing, I have excluded all reference to
other organisations from the first section in order to provide a
clear statement of the fundamental principles. In the second
section, I have left such references in because they help to
clarify the central importance of distinguishing between representative, accountable and democratic organisations of disabled
people and of recognising those who are not.

In what follows the Disablement Income Group is referred
to as DIG and the Disability Alliance as the Alliance. CCD also
appears as this was the Central Council for the Disabled which
later became the Royal Association for Disability and Rehabilitation (RADAR). Those interested in locating what follows properly in its historical context should consult the full document
and Finkelstein recently provided a discussion of this (see Oliver
ed, 1991, pp. 19–31)

### (a) A Statement of Fundamental Principles
The social problem of the poverty of physically impaired
people requires for its solution the same intellectual rigour
as any other problem which is approached scientifically, not
less. The approach of the Union of the Physically Impaired
has clearly demonstrated that disabled people do not need

to be talked down to in 'lay terms'. On the contrary, when
we seriously address ourselves to the problems of our own
social situation, we are capable of rapidly developing an expert
approach. Even in its infancy, the clarity and consistency of
the Union's approach makes an important break with the
traditional amateurish 'spontaneity' encouraged by the Alliance. Our approach helps to clear the confusion that the
'experts' introduce into what is basically a straightforward
issue, requiring the application of fundamental principles,
drawn from the actual experience of disability, rather than
the adoption of 'a very complicated position'.

The Union maintains that, far from being too concerned
with the cause of disability, the 'experts' in the field have
never concerned themselves with the real cause at all. The
fact that they had delusions that they were looking at the
cause, when they were typically concentrating on its effects,
on confusing disability with physical impairment, underlines
the imperative need for disabled people to become their
own experts. It is only when we begin to grasp this expertise
that disabled people will be able to see through the 'expert' attempt to disguise as something 'entirely different'
the traditional, clearly failed, 'spontaneous' struggle against
aspects of disability, such as poverty.

*(b) The Poverty of the Incomes Approach*
. . In our view, it is society which disables physically impaired people. Disability is something imposed on top of
our impairments by the way we are unnecessarily isolated
and excluded from full participation in society. Disabled
people are therefore an oppressed group in society. To understand this it is necessary to grasp the distinction between
the physical impairment and the social situation, called 'disability', of people with such impairment. Thus we define
impairment as lacking part of or all of a limb, or having a
defective limb, organ or mechanism of the body; and disability as the disadvantage or restriction of activity caused
by a contemporary social organisation which takes no or little account of people who have physical impairments and
thus excludes them from participation in the mainstream of
social activities. Physical disability is therefore a particular
form of social oppression.

From this social point of view it follows that the impoverishment of physically impaired people arises out of the fact that, as a group, we are excluded from the mainstream of social activities. In the final analysis the particular form of poverty principally associated with physical impairment is caused by our exclusion from the ability to earn an income on a par with our able-bodied peers, due to the way employment is organised. This exclusion is linked with our exclusion from participating in the social activities and provisions that make general employment possible. For example, physically impaired school children are characteristically excluded from normal education preparatory to work, we are unable to achieve the same flexibility in using transport and finding suitable housing so as to live conveniently to our possible employment, and so on. The need to make a full analysis of the organisation of society is most pressing as this leads to the very essence of disability and its poverty aspect. It is clear that our social organisation does not discriminate equally against all physical impairments and hence there arises the appearance of degrees of exclusion (degrees of disability). For example, people having mild visual impairments (wearing glasses) are doubtless not more impoverished than their visually unimpaired peers. Our social organisation does not exclude people using glasses to the same extent that it excludes people who are blind, or deaf, or cannot speak, or who have brain damage, or who use wheelchairs. Nevertheless, it is the same society which disables people whatever their type, or degree of physical impairment, and therefore there is a single cause within the organisation of society that is responsible for the creation of the disability of physically impaired people. Understanding the cause of disability will enable us to understand the situation of those less affected, as well as helping us to prevent getting lost in the details of the degrees of oppression at the expense of focusing on the essence of the problem.

A crucial factor in this coming together, this growing social identification amongst disabled people, and hence the realisation of a social cause of disability, is that in the last fifty years or so developments in modern technology have made it increasingly possible to employ even the most severely physically impaired people and to integrate us into the mainstream of social and economic activity. . . . The Union's social theory of disability, itself a product of the technological changes in society, reflects the most advanced developments which make it clear that the alternative to an 'incomes' (or more properly, 'pensions') approach to the particular poverty in disability is to struggle for changes to the organisation of society so that employment and full social participation are made accessible to all people, including those with physical impairments. Setting 'incomes' in the context of this struggle, to change the organisation of society, would help physically impaired people recognise the correct emphasis to be placed upon incomes. To avoid retreating in the face of DIG's failed incomes campaign it is necessary to go forward with the serious struggle for the right to paid, integrated employment and full participation in the mainstream of life.

Of course the Union supports and struggles for increased help for physically impaired people, there can be no doubt about our impoverishment and the need for urgent change. However, our Union's Aims seek the 'necessary financial. . . . and other help required from the State to enable us to gain the maximum possible independence in daily living activities, to achieve mobility, undertake productive work and to live where and how we choose with full control over our own lives'. Financial and other help is placed here in relation to the achievement of independence and integration into ordinary employment. This is the fundamental principle by which schemes for meeting the financial and other needs of disabled people can be judged. This means that for people of working age financial and other forms of help must above all be geared to the retention or achievement of integrated employment: dependence on the State must increasingly give way to the provision of help so that a living can be earned through employment. Similarly, the assistance given to physically impaired children must be directed towards their progressive integration into ordinary employment. And for physically impaired people of all ages, the financial and other special help required to meet the extra costs and problems of living with impairments must increasingly be replaced by arrangements which include us as an integral part of society – for example, fully accessible and reliable public transport.

'Benefits' which are not carefully related to the struggle for integrated employment and active social participation will constantly be used to justify our dependence and exclusion from the mainstream of life – the very opposite of what is intended. This is why the . . . appeal to the state for legislation to implement a comprehensive, national disability incomes scheme is in reality nothing so much as a programme to obtain and maintain in perpetuity the historical dependence of physically impaired people on charity. It does not even have the merit of revealing to the public it wishes to educate that its incomes policy is really a form of State Charity – that is, help which essentially entrenches our dependence on the state instead of encouraging our independence and active participation in the mainstream of life. The . . . appeal to the public on our behalf is still the same old appeal to pity, the begging bowl in modern form. A hundred years ago such an appeal for state rather than personal or voluntary charity might have made some sense. But today, when technological and social changes have radically altered the possibilities for us to take independent control over our own lives, to continue to stress our incapacity and helplessness is to bind us with more chains instead of emancipating us. What we really need is to be helped to make our maximum active contribution to society as full members.

. . . the struggle to achieve integration into ordinary employment is the most vital part of the struggle to change the organisation of society so that physically impaired people are no longer impoverished through exclusion from full participation. Only when all physically impaired people of working age are as a matter of course helped to make whatever contribution they can in ordinary work situations, will secure foundations for full integration in society as a whole be laid. All the other situations from which physically impaired people as a whole (including children and those over retirement age) and the lack of positive help for us all to participate fully in areas of life outside employment, can only be systematically and successfully struggled against when this connection is grasped.

It is obvious that this struggle requires a major rethinking of old attitudes and ideas about the social roles of disabled people. It will be necessary to draw the mass of disabled people (of whatever age or type of physical impairment) into the great movement to raise our consciousness of our social identity. A general mass movement of disabled people, and

our increasing integration into normal work and other social situations, will radically improve our social status as a
group. Experts begging for state charity on our behalf can
do nothing but lower our status, by reinforcing out-of-date
attitudes ... The struggle for the right to employment and
full social participation, that is, to eliminate disability and
its poverty aspect, of necessity requires our active involvement. If the mass of disabled people do not engage in this
struggle we will not develop the physical and mental capacity to meet the active demands of employment and other
integrated situations.

   Once the struggle for incomes and benefits is divorced
from the struggle to make employment and the other related areas of life accessible, the involvement of disabled
people is no longer required. The campaign to provide more
charity (whatever it is called) requires only a small group of
'experts' who know the laws, who are recognised as 'authorities' on the subject, and who have detailed schemes for
negotiation. None of this requires any attempt actively to
educate physically impaired people, nor to raise our level of
social awareness. On the contrary, the struggle of a small
group of people for 'authority' on incomes means turning
their backs on our needs while they concentrate on parliament. It is not only that the so-called 'experts' suffer a poverty
of thinking, but also that this narrow approach impoverishes
the intellectual development of disabled people in our own
struggle by continuing to isolate us from the social and ideological developments of our time.

*(c) Raising an Umbrella against the Storm*
The past decade has seen a growing storm of criticism of
the way society treats physically impaired people. This storm
built up during the passing of the Chronically Sick and Disabled Persons Act (1970), and culminated in the failure of
DIG's incomes campaign. It was in this period and subsequently that there was a growing need for our criticism to
be sharpened and directed into the correct channels. At the
same time as we were presented with this challenge for greater
understanding the Alliance 'spontaneously' set about raising its umbrella against the storm. The Union maintains that
the umbrella structure serves to prevent the development
of clear thinking just at the time when this is most needed.

Basing itself on the struggle to achieve State Charity, even in the light of DIG's failed incomes campaign, the Alliance has 'spontaneously' seen more consistently than DIG the way to organise for this purpose. Since the incomes approach does not require the active participation of disabled people (in fact, dealing with our grumbles may take much time away from the 'experts' single-minded concentration on the incomes issue), it is more logical to do away with the active membership. At the same time, the incomes 'experts' cannot completely ignore the disabled population, because this is necessary today to help establish their 'authority' in talks with the Government and in 'education' of the public. The ideal formal structure, then, for organising around the incomes content of DIG, is one that can establish a legitimate distance between the 'expert' leaders and the 'amateur' ordinary members. The answer is 'a federation of organisations' which, unlike DIG and the CCD, they claim, acts 'in an executive capacity' and reflects its wider representation in the subject matter of its pamphlets. This frees the incomes 'experts' from the cumbrance of dealing directly with disabled people and at the same time allows them to claim 'authority' through the membership of the constituent organisations (which are then left to deal with the problem of what to do with their members). This amounts to no less than the willingness of the incomes 'experts' to use disabled people to give authority to their own social interests. That they can use people in this way is frankly demonstrated when they say that the original use of many other experts by the Alliance 'was really just to give dignity to an exchange of correspondence with the Prime Minister' – a remark which, less than flattering to the other experts, says even more of the Alliance's real attitude to disabled people. It would be folly for us to have any confidence in such an organisation which can 'use' people in this manner. The tendency, then, of separating incomes 'experts' from those they claim to represent was initially built into DIG by its organising around the single issue and is now completed in the structure of the Alliance. Far from this being a new approach, the Alliance has carried the weakness in DIG to its logical and consistent organisational level.

The way this separation between the 'experts' and the

'amateurs' works can be demonstrated when we look at the production of the Alliance's educational pamphlets. A relatively tiny group of individuals write, discuss and print pamphlets advocating State Charity. These are then circulated to the public in the name of disabled people before we have had a chance to evaluate their contents critically. The mass of DIG members, for example, were not consulted about the contents of the Alliance's pamphlet, 'Poverty and Disability', which, because of DIG's membership of the Alliance they found themselves ostensibly supporting. The Alliance, by a neat organisational trick, is able to disclaim responsibility for the lack of consultation of physically impaired people. 'We are,' they told us, 'at least consulting other organisations of and for the disabled. We don't have individual members, this is the point.' The point being (quite correctly) that the Alliance does not have the responsibility for consulting physically impaired people, as this lies with the constituent organisations – in our example, with DIG, who must bear the responsibility for bringing their disabled members into such an organisation as the Alliance. By its umbrella structure the Alliance of amateurs is able to render harmless and shelter from any storm of criticism levelled at its State Charity approach. The 'experts' have expertly protected themselves from direct contact with the mass of disabled people, while at the same time they claim to speak for us.

We need not despair, however, of having an effective say in our own affairs. The umbrella is full of holes.

To reiterate the importance of the Fundamental Principles document, there are two points I would wish to draw out from the above. Firstly, the distinction that the first section makes between impairment and disability remains valid to this day and continues to inform the critique that disabled people provided of the subsequent work of OPCS (Abberley 1991) as well as becoming central to the operational definitions adopted by DPI and BCODP. Secondly, the distinctions developed between experts and amateurs and between organisations controlled by disabled people and those not, have shaped the development of the disability movement ever since. These are issues which will be returned to in the final two chapters.

The next chapter discusses the social model of disability which, in my formulation at least, emerged out of the Fundamental Principles document (Oliver 1983) and owes a debt to it. It is for this reason that these two chapters are sequenced historically rather than putting a discussion of the social model first.

# 3
# The Social Model in Context

## Introduction

As one of the originators of discussions about disability models, it is important that I clarify some of the issues I intended to raise when I began to write about the individual and social models of disability as I saw them (Oliver 1983). Before so doing, it is necessary to state at the outset however, that in claiming parental rights to disability models, I am not seeking personal aggrandizement nor indeed to deny the very real contribution that other disabled people have made to opening up the issue, notably Finkelstein (1980).

I originally conceptualised models of disability as the binary distinction between what I chose to call the individual and social models of disability (Oliver 1983). This was no amazing new insight on my part dreamed up in some ivory tower but was really an attempt to enable me to make sense of the world for my social work students and other professionals whom I taught. The idea of the individual and the social model was taken quite simply and explicitly from the distinction originally made between impairment and disability by the Union of the Physically

Impaired Against Segregation in the Fundamental Principles document (1976).

I wanted to put this distinction into a framework that could be understood by professionals with a limited though expanding knowledge of disability issues. The individual model for me encompassed a whole range of issues and was underpinned by what I called the personal tragedy theory of disability. But it also included psychological and medical aspects of disability; the latter being what I preferred, and still prefer, to call the medicalisation rather than the medical model of disability (Manning and Oliver 1985). In short, for me, there is no such thing as the medical model of disability, there is instead, an individual model of disability of which medicalisation is one significant component.

The articulation of this new view of disability did not receive universal acceptance. Originally, it was professionals, policy makers and staff from organisations for disabled people who, because they had vested interests in maintaining the status quo underpinned by the individual model, questioned the experiential validity and explanatory reliability of the social model. However, we have seen a paradigm shift and many professionals have now come to espouse the social model, in theory at least (DHSS 1988, CCETSW 1992). Whether it has had much impact on practice is another question altogether.

The articulation of the social model was received much more enthusiastically by disabled people because it made an immediate connection to their own experiences. It quickly became the basis for disability awareness and later disability equality training. So successful did it become that we saw a proliferation of other models. No longer did we just have the individual and social models; we had the medical, psychological, charity and later the administrative models. At one point it seemed that we would end up with more models than the Lucy Clayton Modelling Agency. Alongside this proliferation of different models disabled people themselves have begun to question the explanatory power of the social model. I myself questioned the way the social model was becoming a straight jacket for our experience in the original version of this Chapter, which was a talk I gave to the annual course for disability equality trainers organised by Jane Campbell and Kath Gillespie-Sells of the Disability Resource Team in 1989.

This aroused a great deal of anger amongst some of the

course participants but, quite rightly, the questioning has continued. This questioning has not attempted to deny the value
of the social model but rather to suggest that while it may
connect with some of the experiences of disabled people, it
does not connect with all of them (French 1993). Further, its
explanatory power has also been questioned (Morris 1991, Crow
1992); while it may partially explain the social oppression of
disabled people, it cannot fully explain it (Finkelstein 1991).

In this chapter, I want to address some of these important
issues and question some of the questions that have been raised
about the social model. I shall initially restate what I see to be
the essential differences between the individual and social models
of disability before going on to clarify the fundamental distinction between illness and disability and to suggest that it is
crucial that we continue to reject the medicalisation of disability, not just in practice but in theory too. I shall then attempt to engage with some of the important questions disabled
people have recently been raising about the social model of
disability. Finally, I will suggest that 'our child' – the social
model – is not yet grown up and that if we turn her out into
the world too soon, we do so at both our and her peril.

## Individual and social models

There are two fundamental points that need to be made about
the individual model of disability. Firstly, it locates the 'problem' of disability within the individual and secondly it sees the
causes of this problem as stemming from the functional limitations or psychological losses which are assumed to arise from
disability. These two points are underpinned by what might be
called 'the personal tragedy theory of disability' which suggests
that disability is some terrible chance event which occurs at
random to unfortunate individuals. Of course, nothing could
be further from the truth.

The genesis, development and articulation of the social model
of disability by disabled people themselves is a rejection of all
of these fundamentals (Oliver 1990). It does not deny the problem of disability but locates it squarely within society. It is not
individual limitations, of whatever kind, which are the cause
of the problem but society's failure to provide appropriate services and adequately ensure the needs of disabled people are
fully taken into account in its social organisation.

Hence disability, according to the social model, is all the things that impose restrictions on disabled people; ranging from individual prejudice to institutional discrimination, from inaccessible public buildings to unusable transport systems, from segregated education to excluding work arrangements, and so on. Further, the consequences of this failure do not simply and randomly fall on individuals but systematically upon disabled people as a group who experience this failure as discrimination institutionalised throughout society.

The social model itself can be located within the original UPIAS definition which bears repeating here.

> In our view it is society which disables physically impaired people. Disability is something imposed on top of our impairments by the way we are unnecessarily isolated and excluded from full participation in society. Disabled people are therefore an oppressed group in society.
>
> (UPIAS 1976, p. 14)

This definition was adopted in modified form by Disabled Peoples International hence ensuring the international influence of the work of UPIAS.

It would be possible to devote the rest of this chapter, and much more, to discussing differences between individual and social models but neither time nor space will allow and I have done this elsewhere (Oliver 1983, 1989, c). Instead, Table 2.1 below summarises some of these differences. It should be noted that, like all tables, this one oversimplifies a complex reality and each item should be seen as the polar end of a continuum. Nevertheless, underpinning it is the fundamental distinction between impairment and disability as defined by UPIAS in the previous chapter.

## Questioning the social model from the outside – the medicalisation of disability

Central to this issue is the question of whether there is a useful or valid distinction between illness and disability. Certainly a number of people, including medical sociologists and policy researchers have questioned this distinction suggesting that the two are interrelated. They argue that the concept of 'social handicap' which was introduced in the mid 1960s and sub-

TABLE 2.1   *Disability models*

| The individual model | The social model |
| --- | --- |
| personal tragedy theory | social oppression theory |
| personal problem | social problem |
| individual treatment | social action |
| medicalisation | self-help |
| professional dominance | individual and collective responsibility |
| expertise | experience |
| adjustment | affirmation |
| individual identity | collective identity |
| prejudice | discrimination |
| attitudes | behaviour |
| care | rights |
| control | choice |
| policy | politics |
| individual adaptation | social change |

sequently incorporated both into the first national survey of disabled people (Harris 1971) and the International Classification of Impairments, Disabilities and Handicaps (WHO 1980), refers to what disabled people call disability. In other words WHO's definition of social handicap is the same as UPIAS's definition of disability.

This claim has not been accepted by disabled people and has led to conflicts between social scientists seeking to classify the disabled population and map the dimensions of disadvantage they faced and disabled people struggling to develop a collective identity and overcome the disadvantages they face. Partly as a consequence of these early conflicts, the medical sociology of chronic illness and social theorising about disability developed into two separate and occasionally hostile camps. While each may have influenced the other to some extent, this influence has rarely been acknowledged. Nonetheless, both camps have now produced impressive bodies of work, incorporating both academic scholarship and substantial empirical research.

The two areas where these conflicts have emerged are epistemological and methodological. In epistemological terms, the crucial issue is that of causality. For medical sociologists, what they call chronic illness is causally related to the disadvantages disabled people experience. For the social model however, there is no causal link; disability is wholly and exclusively social. Hence each side accuses the other of being incorrect in causal terms. It may well be, however, that this debate is in reality the result of terminological rather than epistemological confusion; that the real similarities exist between chronic illness and impairment.

Thus one medical sociologist critically argues

Sometimes, in seeking to reject the reductionism of the medical model and its institutional contexts, proponents of independent living have tended to discuss disablement as if it had nothing to do with the physical body.

(Williams 1991, p. 521)

Ironically that is precisely what the social model insists, disablement is nothing to do with the body. It is a consequence of social oppression. But the social model does not deny that impairment is closely related to the physical body. Impairment is, in fact, nothing less than a description of the physical body.

This terminological confusion also appeared when a policy analyst attempted to relate her own experience to policy issues in the area of disability.

I found myself puzzled by arguments that held that disability had nothing to do with illness or that belief in a need for some form of personal adaptation to impairment was essentially a form of false consciousness. I knew that disabled people argue that they should not be treated as if they were ill, but could see that many people who had impairments as a result of ongoing illness were also disabled. My unease increased as I watched my parents coming to terms with my mother's increasing impairments (and disability) related to arterial disease which left her tired and in almost continual pain. I could see that people can be disabled by their physical, economic and social environment but I could also see that people who became disabled (rather than being born with impairments) might have to renegotiate their sense of themselves both with themselves and with those closest to them.

(Parker 1993, p. 2)

The social model does not deny that some illnesses may have disabling consequences and many disabled people have illnesses at various points in their lives. Further, it may be entirely appropriate for doctors to treat illnesses of all kinds, though even here, the record of the medical profession is increasingly coming under critical scrutiny. Leaving this aside however, doctors can have a role to play in the lives of disabled people: stabilising their initial condition, treating any illnesses which may arise and which may or may not be disability related.

The problem arises when doctors try to use their knowledge and skills to treat disability rather than illness. Disability as a long-term social state is not treatable medically and is certainly not curable. Hence many disabled people experience much medical intervention as, at best, inappropriate, and, at worst, oppressive. This should not be seen as a personal attack on individual doctors, or indeed the medical profession, for they, too, are trapped in a set of social relations with which they are not trained or equipped to deal.

The problem is that doctors are socialised by their own training into believing that they are 'experts' and accorded that role by society. When confronted with the social problems of disability as experts, they cannot admit that they don't know what to do. Consequently they feel threatened and fall back on their medical skills and training, inappropriate as they are, and impose them on disabled people. They then appear bewildered when disabled people criticise or reject this imposed treatment.

Of course, one could pursue this image of doctors as threatened and bewildered too far. As society's experts, they have a great deal of power and this gives them control over fundamental aspects of people's lives and they have not been noticeably reticent about using this power to make decisions about disabled people's lives; where they should live, whether they should work or not, what kind of school they should go to, what kinds of benefits and services they should receive and in the case of unborn disabled children, whether they should live or not.

However, it's not just decisions that doctors make about disabled people that are questionable; it's also about what they do to them. The whole medical and rehabilitation enterprise is founded upon an ideology of normality and this has far reaching implications for rehabilitation and treatment (see Chapter 7 for a further discussion of this). Its aim is to restore the disabled person to normality, whatever that may mean. Where that is not possible, the basic aim is not abandoned; the goal is to restore the disabled person to a state that is as near normality as possible. So, surgical intervention and physical rehabilitation, whatever its costs in terms of the pain and suffering of disabled individuals, is always justified and justifiable – the ideology of normality rules.

Further, the medical profession, because of its power and dominance, has spawned a whole range of pseudo-professions in its own image; physiotherapy, occupational therapy, speech therapy, clinical psychology; each one geared to the same aim – the restoration of normality. And each one of these pseudo-professions develops its own knowledge base and set of skills to facilitate this. They organise their interventions and intrusions into disabled peoples' lives on the basis of discreet and limited knowledge and skills.

The reality, of course, is that disabled peoples' lives cannot be divided up in this way to suit professional activity and increasingly, disabled people, individually and collectively, are coming to reject the prescriptions of the 'normalising' society and the whole range of professional activities which attempt to reinforce it.

Instead, we are increasingly demanding acceptance from society as we are, not as society thinks we should be. It is society that has to change not individuals and this change will come about as part of a process of political empowerment of disabled people as a group and not through social policies and programmes delivered by establishment politicians and policy makers nor through individualised treatments and interventions provided by the medical and para-medical professions. This is the core of the social model and its message should not be mystified by conceptual misunderstandings about the meanings of terms like illness and disability.

## Criticising the social model from within

A major criticism that some disabled people have made of the social model concerns the way it connects, or rather doesn't connect with the experience of impairment. French (1993), for example, argues that her visual impairment imposes some social restrictions which cannot be resolved by the application of the principles of social model. She cites as examples her inability to recognise people and read or emit non-verbal cues in social interactions.

Clearly, most disabled people can come up with similar examples. As a wheelchair user when I go to parties I am more restricted than some other people from interacting with everyone else and what's more, it is difficult to see a solution – houses are usually crowded with people during parties and that makes circulation difficult for a wheelchair user. But other people may find circulation difficult as well but for other reasons; they may simply be shy. The point that I am making is that the social model is not an attempt to deal with the personal restrictions of impairment but the social barriers of disability.

Other disabled people have criticised the social model for its assumed denial of 'the pain of impairment', both physical and psychological. In many ways some of these criticisms mirror those made from without although they are not beset by the same terminological confusion between illness and impairment.

> ... there is a tendency within the social model of disability to deny the experience of our own bodies, insisting that our physical differences and restrictions are entirely socially created. While environmental barriers and social attitudes are a crucial part of our experience of disability – and do indeed disable us – to suggest that this is all there is to it is to deny the personal experience of physical or intellectual restrictions, of illness, of the fear of dying.
>
> (Morris 1991, p. 10)

This denial of the pain of impairment has not, in reality, been a denial at all. Rather it has been a pragmatic attempt to identify and address issues that can be changed through collective action rather than medical or other professional treatment.

> If a person's physical pain is the reason they are unhappy then there is nothing the disability movement can do about it. All that BCODP can do is facilitate the politicisation of people around these issues. Of course this politicisation is fairly difficult to make practical progress with – much easier to achieve anti-discrimination legislation than a total review of how society regards death and dying, I imagine. This might explain why these subjects haven't been made a priority, but their day will come.
>
> (Vasey 1992, p. 43)

These criticisms are taken further by Crow (1992) who argues that the way forward for the social model is to fully integrate the experience of impairment with the experience of disability. However, up to now and for very important reasons, the social model has insisted that there is no causal relationship between impairment and disability.

> The achievement of the disability movement has been to break the link between our bodies and our social situation, and to focus on the real cause of disability, i.e. discrimination and prejudice. To mention biology, to admit pain, to confront our impairments, has been to risk the oppressors seizing on evidence that disability is 'really' about physical limitation after all.
>
> (Shakespeare 1992, p. 40)

A further internal criticism comes from other oppressed groups who feel that these other oppressions such as racism (Hill 1992), sexism (Morris 1991) and homophobia (Hearn 1991) have not been incorporated into the social model. Again, it is certainly true that the social model has not explicitly addressed the issue of multiple oppression but then such issues are only just beginning to be explored both in respect of disability (Zarb and Oliver 1993) and race and gender.

This dissatisfaction then, has been expressed not simply because the social model does not adequately reflect experience of oppression of all disabled people but also because it may 'oversimplify' some of the issues raised in Disability Equality Training.

> For some time I have been dissatisfied with the oversimplified 'social model' of disability we are obliged to use in Disability Equality Training and have read with interest the recent arguments re-introducing 'impairment' into that model.
>
> Although the 'social model' has for some time served us well as a way of directing attention away from the personal to the political, I feel now that the debate has been hampered by the rather rigid genealogy of disability thinking. My own literary, linguistic and therapeutic background led me to post-modernist thinkers such as Foucault, Derrida, Barthes and Lacan in an attempt to make sense of the personal and political aspects of the disability debate.
>
> (Cashling 1993, pp. 199–200)

It is undeniably true that some trainers may have used the
social model in an over rigid way, and as I have already argued, I made a similar point in 1989. Those like myself, who
draw on Marxist rather than post-modernist thinking call this
reification; a not uncommon phenomena in late capitalist society. Such criticism however, raises questions about the way
the model is used, rather than the model itself; although, as I
have already suggested, models are merely ways to help us to
better understand the world, or those bits of it under scrutiny.
If we expect models to explain, rather than aid understanding, they are bound to be found wanting. And it remains to be
seen if post-modernist thinking, as Cashling suggests it might,
ends up explaining the oppression of disabled people as simply
a manifestation of society's hatred of us, whether this will take
us as far as the social model in challenging that oppression.

A final criticism comes from another of the founding fathers
of the social model, Vic Finkelstein. Recently (Finkelstein 1991)
he has questioned the ability of the social model to fully explain the social position of disabled people in modern society,
and suggests that there are at least two variants; the social death
model and the social barriers model. He then goes on to suggest that the administrative model is the only one which has
sufficient scope to fully explain societal responses to disabled
people.

> In my view administrative approaches dominate all forms of
> helping services for disabled people in the UK, whether these
> are provided by statutory agencies or voluntary bodies, or
> demanded by pressure group organisations. The cure or care
> forms of intervention are administered within the rehabili-
> tation and personal-care services respectively.
>
> (Finkelstein 1993, p. 37)

Thus, for him, the administrative model subsumes both the
medical and welfare (care) approaches to disability and is centrally concerned with controlling disabled people. For me, the
administrative model is similar to the position I took in trying
to locate disability historically within the rise of capitalist society.

> As the conditions of capitalist production changed in the
> twentieth century, so the labour needs of capital shifted from
> a mass of unskilled workers to a more limited need of skilled

ones. As a result of this, the Welfare State arose as a means of ensuring the supply of skill, and in order to 'pacify' the ever increasing army of the unemployed, the under-employed and the unemployable.

(Manning and Oliver 1985, p. 102)

While I think Finkelstein and I are basically saying the same thing, for me it is important not to stretch the explanatory power of models further than they are able to go. For me the social model of disability is about personal experience and professional practice but it is not a substitute for social theory, a materialist history of disability nor an explanation of the welfare state.

## Conclusions

My argument in this chapter has centred on two key points. Firstly we must not assume that models in general and the social model in particular can do everything; that it can explain disability in totality. It is not a social theory of disability and it cannot do the work of social theory. Secondly, because it cannot explain everything, we should neither seek to expose inadequacies, which are more a product of the way we use it, nor abandon it before its usefulness has been fully exploited.

The social model does connect with the experience of disabled people as the following quote illustrates.

The second flash on this road to Damascus as a disabled person came when I encountered the disability movement. I had learnt to live with my private fear and to feel that I was the only one involved in this fight. I had internalised my oppression. As a working class son of Irish immigrants, I had experienced other struggles but, in retrospect, I evidently saw epilepsy as my hidden cross. I cannot explain how significantly all this was turned around when I came into contact with the notion of the social model of disabilities, rather than the medical model which I had hitherto lived with. Over a matter of months, my discomfort with this secret beast of burden called epilepsy, and my festering hatred at the silencing of myself as a disabled person, 'because I didn't look it', completely changed. I think I went through an almost evangelical conversion as I realised that my disability was not, in fact, the epilepsy, but the toxic drugs with their denied side-effects; the medical regime with its blaming of the victim; the judgement through distance and silence of bus-stop crowds, bar-room crowds and dinner-table friends; the fear; and, not least, the employment problems. All this was the oppression, not the epileptic seizure at which I was hardly (consciously) present.

(Hevey 1992, pp. 1–2)

While it has the power to transform consciousness in the way described above, its demise is surely premature.

In addition it continues to serve as a means for getting professionals to reflect on their own practice.

It was during this period that I discovered the writings of disabled people on the broader nature of disablism and the 'social model of disability' – which provided a theoretical model that was more meaningful to me.

(Stevens 1993, p. 33)

Finally, the continuing use and refinement of the social model can contribute to rather than be a substitute for the development of an adequate social theory of disability. And as both Abberley (1987) and myself (1990) have argued, an adequate social theory of disability must contain a theory of impairment. But they are not interchangeable and should not be treated as such as one recent commentator does.

The social model of disability appears to have been constructed for healthy quadriplegics. The social model avoids mention of pain, medication or ill-health".

(Humphrey 1994, p. 6)

The social model of disability does, indeed avoid mention of such things, not because it was written by healthy quadriplegics, but because they properly belong within the social model of impairment. So let's develop a social model of impairment to stand alongside a social model of disability but let's not pretend that either or both are social theory.

# 4
# Citizenship, Welfare and Community Care

## Introduction

In the previous chapter I discussed the influence the social model has had not simply on the consciousness of disabled people but also on welfare provision and professional practice. In this chapter I shall focus on another 'big idea', that of citizenship. I shall consider it in the context of the re-structuring of state welfare that is currently going on and consider its problems and potential in respect of disabled peoples' struggles to live independently.

My interest in welfare in general and community care in particular stems from three sources. Firstly, there is my own experience as a recipient of welfare and the struggles I have experienced to live the kind of life I choose. Secondly, there is my professional interest in welfare services stemming from working in a social services department and in providing welfare within disability organisations. Thirdly, as an academic, I have watched in dismay as these services continue to be reorganised on the basis of advice from people who have little or no experience of them and how the advice of service users continues to be ignored.

This chapter then is a distillation of my own views as they have developed over the years; earlier versions were presented to a Social Services Policy Forum seminar and written as part of the new Open University course 'The Disabling Society'. This version is an attempt to provide a historical account of the relationship between welfare services and disabled people as well as to consider the limits and possibilities of the most recent legislative changes.

## Why citizenship?

The notion of citizenship has become fashionable once again and has become a shorthand device for talking about the relationship between individuals and their societies. Why we should rediscover citizenship at the end of the twentieth century is an interesting question in itself. It seems that when the relationship between the State and its population is in crisis, citizenship becomes the device whereby such a crisis is talked about and mediated. Hence, such a crisis occurred in the nineteenth century, was discussed in terms of citizenship and was eventually resolved through the extension of the franchise to increasing numbers of political citizens. After the Second World War, another crisis emerged and was resolved through the establishment of a welfare state and the consequent emergence of social citizenship. As we move towards the twenty-first century, another crisis between the state and its citizens is emerging.

Whether it can or will be resolved is beyond the scope of this chapter. Instead I shall consider what this rediscovery of the concept of citizenship means for disabled people in general and, in particular, what implications it might have for the provision of state welfare. While politicians, policy makers and professionals have rediscovered the notion of citizenship, disabled people have begun to redefine disability not as personal tragedy requiring therapy but as collective oppression requiring political action. Thus, for the former group, the history of citizenship can be seen as the achievement of certain political, social and civil rights for everyone. For the latter, disability is nothing less than the denial of basic human rights to certain groups within society.

Until recently, there was general consensus that, except for a few unfortunate minority groups or individuals, British citizenship meant for the vast majority of British citizens the achievement of these rights. However the 1980s saw the fracturing of the cosy post-war political and social consensus to the point where people of all political persuasions are seeking to reclaim the idea of citizenship.

> Commentators from all political persuasions lay claim to some definition of citizenship. The traditional liberal view is based upon individual rights based in legislation, whilst the New Right locate individual 'freedoms' not in law but in the choice to operate more in the 'informal' or private spheres than in state institutions. A new development of the Left is a definition of citizenship based upon need. This is informed by an appreciation of 'difference', and underlined by an understanding of societal power and how certain groups such as black people, people with a disability, and women, have been marginalised.
>
> (Taylor and Bishop 1991, p. 5)

Before considering this in the context of disability, a brief history of the concept of citizenship as applied to disabled people, needs to be outlined.

## History of citizenship

In the late nineteenth century, citizenship was the concept used by many philosophers and social theorists to describe the political integration of people into their societies. As more and more groups were given the vote, the concept of citizenship receded into the background. It was briefly revived in the middle of the twentieth century through the influential work of T. H. Marshall (1951). According to him, the history of citizenship can be seen as the achievement of certain rights; these he divided up into political, social and civil rights. The achievement of these rights was evidence of the way all were integrated into British society, he argued.

In recent years, the idea of citizenship has been used not simply to consider the social integration of the majority into society but also as a yardstick to measure the extent to which certain groups are not socially integrated. One example of this is the poor and the relationship between poverty and citizenship. Lister (1991) has recently pointed out that we are in danger of entering the twenty-first century with a growing number of people being excluded from the full enjoyment of the rights of citizenship. She goes on to argue that

> it is time to go on the offensive and restate the case for effective citizenship rights for all, regardless of class, race, gender, age, disability or employment status.
>
> (Lister 1991, p. 2)

Before arguing for effective citizenship rights for disabled people, it is necessary to demonstrate that, at present, disabled people are not citizens, at least, not in Marshall's definition of the term.

## Political rights

It is commonly assumed that universal suffrage in Britain has been achieved but it has recently been shown that many disabled people are denied the opportunity to exercise their political choice through the ballot box. Some disabled people do not enjoy this right because they do not appear on the electoral register for a whole variety of reasons (Ward 1987; MIND 1990). Others who do appear are denied the opportunity to exercise political choice because of problems of access (Spastics Society 1992); access to polling stations, access to transport to take people there or access to information to make an informed choice (Fry 1987; Barnes 1991).

The existence of postal and proxy voting systems do not resolve these problems for the machinery of obtaining access to these systems is complex and confusing. In addition it entails voting before everyone else and hence making decisions before everyone else and before campaigning is completed.

There are a number of other ways in which disabled people find it difficult to participate in the political process, not solely concerned with voting. To begin with, many local political parties hold their meetings in inaccessible premises and hence joining a political party is often not without difficulty. In addition, few political meetings provide signing facilities and little thought is given to making political information accessible to people with visual impairments.

Even if these difficulties are overcome, campaigning is difficult for oneself or on behalf of others, because of difficulties in the physical and communication environments. Hence there are very few disabled people who are active at the party political level either within local or central government. It has been suggested that party politics have failed disabled people and further, that they have been inadequately supported by voluntary organisations and single issue pressure groups purporting to act on their behalf (Oliver and Zarb 1989; Oliver 1990).

## Social rights

In talking about social rights to citizenship, Marshall's own definition is an appropriate yardstick to consider whether disabled people can claim to be social citizens.

> By the social element I mean the whole range from the right to a modicum of economic welfare and security to the right to share to the full in the social heritage and to live the life of a civilised being, according to the standard prevailing in the society
>
> (Marshall 1952, p. 11)

Hence there are a number of elements to Marshall's notion of social citizenship; notably the right not to be poor or live in fear of poverty, to use social facilities in the same way as everyone else and to have a standard of living or lifestyle compatible with current social expectations.

In none of these elements can it be argued that disabled people share the rights to social citizenship. In terms of poverty, the Government's own figures (Martin and White 1988) show over 4 million disabled people being reliant on social security benefits and hence living below the official poverty line. Further it has been suggested that these figures underestimate the nature and extent of poverty amongst disabled people (Thompson *et al.* 1990).

Even using the Governments own figures, no less than two thirds of the total population of disabled people are living in poverty. If such a figure was reproduced in the rest of the population, there would be 40 million people living in poverty; hardly conducive to the functional integration of individuals into society or to the stability of social order. Finally, when freedom from the fear of poverty is considered to be a right of social citizenship, and Marshall certainly considered that it was, then very few disabled people would be in this position.

On top of this, social rights to use the same facilities as everyone else are not accorded to disabled people, whether these be rights to move around the built environment, to travel on transport systems which claim to be public or to have access to public information of all kinds, because usually it is only produced in spoken or written English.

Finally, in many areas of their lives, disabled peoples' experiences do not accord with the lifestyle expectations of their contemporaries. For example, many disabled adults do not have the right to decide what time to get up or go to bed, or indeed who to go to bed with, when or what to eat, how often to bath or even be in control of the times when they empty their bladders or open their bowels.

## Civil rights

For Marshall, civil rights went beyond a narrow conception of legal rights and included not only property rights and the right of contract but also rights to the freedoms of thought and speech, religious practice, and of assembly and association. In theory, disabled people are accorded these basic civil rights although in things like the right of contract, they may experience severe difficulties; in buying goods on hire purchase, taking out a mortgage or obtaining life insurance for example. Those disabled people living in residential establishments may also experience a denial in terms of their rights to freedom of assembly and association.

In the narrower area of legal rights, there are a number of ways in which disabled people are disadvantaged. Where they do have legal rights, as in the Disabled Persons (Employment) Act 1944, which was supposed to give disabled people equal access to job opportunities, these are usually not enforced. Hence despite the fact that over 70 per cent of firms do not meet their legal obligations under this Act, there have only been ten prosecutions since 1944. In other areas, legal regulation, usually through the operation of by-laws, are used to deny disabled people the right to use facilities that other people take for granted, such as using the London underground or many cinemas.

Finally, in some areas, disabled people are denied legal rights accorded to other groups. This occurs most notably in terms of legal rights not to be discriminated against, a right accorded to black people and women; although having such a right does not mean that discrimination disappears. Hence, despite the recommendation of a major report (CORAD 1982) and at least a dozen attempts to introduce anti-discrimination legislation, at the time of writing, no such law has reached the statute books although its eventual successful passage is, in my view, inevitable.

Failing to achieve full citizenship rights may call into question the idea of citizenship as a means to the social integration of individuals into society in that it

> is rooted in a conception of what it is to be a full member of a community and the social rights that are necessary to protect and reinforce that membership.
>
> (Marshall 1952, p. 11)

## The duties and obligations of citizenship

So far we have considered the rights to citizenship and suggested that disabled people are not accorded the full range of rights we accord to citizens. However, all definitions of citizenship consider duties and obligations as well as rights and entitlements.

> The law places on citizens a wide range of duties, including obedience to the criminal law and such civil laws as the laws of negligence and contract. Whilst personal moral codes may differ, the law sets out a common code of conduct binding on all members of society.
>
> The duties, responsibilities and rights of citizenship are defined within a framework of national and international law. They include such basic human rights as freedom of thought, belief and expression, freedom of association, freedom from discrimination on the grounds of race or sex, the right to a fair trial and to the due processes of law. They also include rights to which citizens are entitled by virtue of the laws of particular countries, such as consumer and employment rights.
>
> (NCC 1990, p. 8)

Having suggested that at one level citizenship is nothing more or less than a shorthand device to consider the relationship between individuals and society, the precise nature of that relationship is clearly a complex one. One of those complexities is that the relationship is not one-dimensional; as well as providing rights and entitlements, citizenship also imposes duties and obligations. Another complexity is the fact that definitions of citizenship are influenced both by the historical circumstances and the current context in which they are formulated. A final complexity concerns the ways in which national and international laws influence these formulations of citizenship.

Definitions of the duties and obligations of citizenship are also influenced by current political ideologies. Hence the left have tended to portray the idea of citizenship as the obligations of the state to its citizenry. The duties and obligations of the citizen are thus seen as the contribution of the individual to the collective welfare of all. The right, on the other hand, has tended to portray the idea of citizenship as protection of the individual from the intrusions of the state; hence the development of the idea of the active citizenship and the proposing of a citizens' charter. The duties and obligations of the active citizen are to contribute to their own individual welfare because, only in this way, can the welfare of all be maximised.

However, neither collectivist nor individualistic notions have been wholly successful for

> Citizenship has not been realised for excluded groups either through the false collectivism of social democratic welfare, or through the consumerist democracy of the market.
>
> (Taylor 1989, p. 19)

As already mentioned the poverty of disabled people, their lack of access to public transport, housing, employment etc., can be regarded as evidence of this lack of success of either collectivist or individualistic approaches to welfare. And the same case can be made in respect of people with learning difficulties (Walmsley 1991).

Earlier I spent some time considering Marshall's work on citizenship. This work was not uninfluenced by his concern to show that post-war Britain, despite the advent of the welfare state, was still a class-based society; hence his major work was entitled *Citizenship and Social Class*. According to Lister (1990, p. 31), this preoccupation with class has tended to obscure ways in which citizenship participation has been limited by other important determinants of social position, such as gender, race and disability.

The extent to which Britain, despite laws to the contrary, remains a racist and sexist society has been established by a number of studies (Gregory 1987, Smith 1989). Again citizenship has become the mechanism for talking about the relationship between women and society and black people and society. Hence

social relations must be situated in the context of underlying power based not only on property but on 'race' and gender as well. These power relations structure the spaces of the market and the state and thus limit the extent to which either can fulfil the ideal of citizenship.

(Taylor 1989, p. 19)

In other words, just as with disabled people, both black people and women have been denied access to the full rights of citizenship on account of race and gender in just the same ways as disabled people have been denied access on account of impairment. And again, as with disabled people, the welfare state has compounded this in respect of race and gender (Williams 1989).

The situation is further complicated by the need to consider citizenship in respect of people who are part of more than one oppressed group. In an analysis of the experiences of disabled women, Morris (1989, 1991) forcibly makes this point referring not just to women, but black disabled people and disabled gay men and lesbians whose 'experiences . . . should not be treated as an 'added on' optional extra to more general analysis of disability' (Morris 1991, p. 12).

We lack systematic evidence to enable us to talk in any detail about this relationship between groups who are oppressed in more than one way although a conceptual framework which allows such experiences to be seen as simultaneous oppression is beginning to emerge (Morris 1992, Stuart 1992). In a recent study on ageing and disability, I and a colleague concluded that

Although it is clear that older disabled people have no wish to demand any more than they need to maintain control over their own lives, the combination of ageism, disablism and other forms of oppression . . . . . means that many are forced into a life of dependency and denied even the most basic rights of citizenship.

(Zarb and Oliver 1993, p. 131)

At this point it is necessary to re-emphasise the theme of citizenship as a way of talking about the relationship of individuals and society, and that definitions of citizenship are not unrelated to this.

Citizenship may be defined in various ways (by reference to civil, legal and social features) but citizenship rights are essentially concerned with the nature of social participation of persons within the community as fully recognised legal members.

(Turner 1986, p. 134)

And it's worth pointing out that social participation in the community may depend on the customs and practices of the community itself. For example, deaf people on Martha's Vineyard, an isolated community off the north American coast, participated fully in their community because everyone there spoke sign language (Groce 1985).

## Citizenship and welfare

It needs to be said at the outset that, had the mammoth and imaginative project to establish a welfare state which would provide 'cradle to grave' security for all its members, been successful, then disabled people would now be accorded many of the rights of citizenship. Further, not only has state welfare not ensured the citizenship rights of disabled people, but through some of its provisions and practices it has infringed and even taken away some of these rights.

Examples of this include the provision of segregated residential facilities such as Young Disabled Units or Cheshire Homes which deny some disabled people the right to live where they choose, not necessarily maliciously but because to live in such an establishment means that individuals are regarded as being adequately housed; consequently there is no statutory duty on the housing authority to house them. The imposition of some assessment procedures deny some disabled people the right to privacy in that they may have to reveal details of all of their financial affairs in order simply to be supplied with an aid to daily living.

Before considering in some detail the reasons for this, it should be pointed out that the idea of a welfare state is compatible with both the idea of collective and active citizenship; collective citizenship implies a universal welfare state, active citizenship a residual one. Neither have served disabled people well, as the rest of this chapter and the next one will show.

When the Speaker's Commission on Citizenship produced its report, it re-affirmed this connection.

> The Commission recommends that a floor of adequate social entitlements should be maintained, monitored and improved when possible by central government with the aim of enabling every citizen to live the life of a civilised human being according to the standards prevailing in society.
>
> (HMSO 1990, p. xix)

This quote makes two points; that there should be minimum standards for everyone and that the services necessary to obtain these minimum standards should be available as of right. It is precisely on these two grounds it can be argued that the welfare state has failed disabled people.

The evidence for the failure to ensure minimum standards is not in dispute and has been provided by officially commissioned government research showing the extent of poverty and unemployment amongst disabled people (Martin and Meltzer 1989); studies by independent research institutes showing that disabled people are 'last on the list' as far as welfare services are concerned (Beardshaw 1988); academics who show that services to enable disabled people to live in the community are poor (Blaxter 1980; Borsay 1986) and disabled people who condemn health authorities and social service departments who fail to provide them with a satisfactory quality of life (Oliver *et al.* 1988; Morris 1989).

What is perhaps more contentious is that there is a connection between the failure to ensure minimum standards and the issue of statutory entitlements. It is certainly true that despite the establishment of a comprehensive legal framework for the provision of services to disabled people, these services somehow do not get delivered (Oliver and Barnes 1991). The main reason for this is because the rights to services enshrined in the original legislation have been subverted and that services have come to be provided on the basis of professional definitions of need instead. The 'problem of need' will be returned to in the next chapter but it remains true that by the end of the 1970s, there was concern from all sides that the welfare state was not functioning as it should.

These concerns can basically be summarised under three issues. Firstly, the costs of state welfare were escalating alarmingly to the point where there was an urgent need to cut public spending and reduce the amount of gross national product (GNP) spent in the public sector. Secondly, the provision of state welfare encouraged the creation of dependency, the existence of a dependency culture. Thirdly, the services that were provided were dominated by and served the interests of the professionals employed in them rather than met the needs of those people who were supposed to benefit.

As a consequence of these concerns the General Election of 1979 saw the coming to power of a Conservative Government committed to major restructuring of the welfare state because it had become over-bureaucratised, resulting in unacceptable costs and lack of choice. The philosophy underlying this was captured in a speech by John Moore, Secretary of State for Social Services at the time;

> One of the most damaging aspects of the myth that the welfare state was created wholly by Labour after 1945, is that it was also created perfect: the ultimate, total, flawless welfare state. So that ever afterwards suggested change of even the most necessary and obvious sort has been greeted with howls of outrage about 'dismantling and destroying'. This is a ridiculous state of affairs . . . Life has changed, needs have changed, people's expectations have changed, and it is necessary for what we call our 'welfare state' to change as well.

The two major pieces of legislation directly concerned with changing state welfare in respect of disability, were the Education Act 1981 which was supposed to add momentum to the integration of disabled children into ordinary schools and the Disabled Persons (Services, Consultation and Representation) Act 1986 which was supposed to give disabled people a voice in the planning, design and delivery of services provided for them. Relatively no more children are being integrated than before the Education Act was passed and important sections of the Disabled Person's Act remain unimplemented.

Neither has added substantially to the citizenship rights of disabled people nor addressed the way in which provision continues to reinforce dependency and professional dominance of state welfare services remains. More recently the Government has decided to restructure the way it provides care in the community and the implications for this need to be considered. Specifically, we need to ask whether this restructuring is likely to assist disabled people in their struggles to live independently.

## Re-thinking community care

Beginning with a damning report on community care from the Audit Commission (1986), the Griffiths Report (DHSS 1988) followed some two years later and after much delay, this was incorporated into a white paper 'Caring for People' (DHS 1990). After a very short consultation period the white paper was incorporated into the National Health Service Act (1990) and discussions about implementation began in earnest. No sooner had these discussions begun however when the Government announced that implementation had been delayed and would be phased in over a longer period and the reforms have only been fully operational since April 1993.

Central to them is a new managerial strategy for providing services which is to be supplemented by a market strategy which involves stimulating the private and voluntary sectors to act as providers of services and for the statutory authorities to act as enablers and purchasers of services rather than sole providers. What this will mean in practice is that health and social services will no longer have to be sole providers. In fact, they will have a duty to purchase welfare services at the cheapest cost commensurate with maintaining appropriate quality.

By opting for this combination of market and managerial strategies, the Government hoped that the problems of professional dominance and dependency creation would be addressed. However, markets are characterised, at least in economic terms, by the balance of power between buyers and sellers. Unfortunately, such a balance does not exist in the social welfare market, given the history of the domination of welfare services by the professionals who provide those services.

This crucial issue has been addressed recently by adopting what might be called 'an empowerment strategy', which has involved the production of a range of charters specifying the rights that people can expect from public services. So far these have included an overall one, the Citizen's Charter, the Patient's Charter in respect of health and the Parent's Charter in respect of education. While these specify the basic standards that people can expect, they are largely silent on how to achieve legal redress if authorities fail to meet these basic standards.

More specifically these charters scarcely mention disability or the citizenship rights of disabled people. This suggests that the Government has explicitly turned away from this empowerment strategy as far as disabled people are concerned. By its lack of commitment to the implementation of the Disabled Persons (1986) Act, its consistent refusal to instigate anti-discrimination legislation and its chronic underfunding of organisations controlled by disabled people, it has clearly shown that while it may want a market in social welfare, it does not want a market where users (as they are now euphemistically being called) have any power.

This view has been further reinforced by the Government's refusal to allow local authorities to make direct payments to disabled people to purchase their own personal assistance services. Instead we have the case manager or the care manager as they have variously been called, who will be responsible for purchasing packages of care on behalf of disabled people within a mixed economy of welfare. Despite intensive political lobbying, the Government has remained firm and will not allow disabled people to purchase their own services within the welfare market.

Thus Davis (1993) comments on the continuing dominance of professionals over service delivery.

> At this juncture, our lives are substantially still in their hands.
> They still determine most decisions and their practical outcomes.
> (Davis 1993, p. 199)

He is not attacking individual professionals but the structure of welfare services which place the power and control of those services in professional hands.

To be fair to the newly emerging profession of care manager, it is not solely seen as a way of addressing the problems already discussed. Care management is also seen as the last in a long line of attempts to cut through the tangles created by agency boundaries and different professional perspectives to arrive at flexible packages of care organised around the needs of individual disabled people. Given that previous attempts including the case conference, the multi-disciplinary team and the named person or key worker have lamentably failed, it seems unlikely the care manager will succeed.

While it is true that a few published studies indicate an improvement in services delivered for those disabled people in receipt of case management (Hunter 1988), it is by no means clear that it can resolve some of the structural and ideological problems of the disabling welfare environment.

> Does the grafting on of new arrangements not reflect a fail-ure of existing services to fulfil their existing remits and does it not serve to postpone or, at worst, pre-empt altogether vigorous attempts to correct these anomalies or management failures? Or, alternatively, are they a sophisticated and necessary adjunct to existing arrangements which, though in theory charged with the task of co-ordinating care, are in practice incapable of operating to secure it.
>
> (Hunter 1988, p. 32)

Davis has recently turned his analytical attention to the care manager and he is equally clear that this newly emerging pro-fession will not provide the necessary structural reforms.

> ... it is simply not enough for brokers, care managers or any other agent to potter about in the existing mish-mash of inappropriate and inadequate services, with a view to helping individual disabled people to piece together some kind of survival plan for existing in a hostile world. We have been there too long.
>
> (Davis 1990, p. 14)

While it is too early to be definitive about the ways in which the restructuring is working, it has to be said that the early signs are not hopeful. There is little evidence that disabled people are being involved in the planning and delivery of services in the way that legislation requires (Bewley and Glendinning 1992, 1994). Nor is there much evidence that local authority assessment procedures adequately reflect the legal requirement to place individual needs at the centre of the reforms (Ellis

1993). Finally, studies that have recently been carried out are not optimistic that the existing reforms are enough and unless further changes are made, as far as disabled people are concerned, 'their opportunities to be independent citizens will disappear' (Morris 1993a, 1993b).

So the welfare state has not ensured either the rights and entitlements of disabled people in the past nor does the current re-structuring appear likely to change this. Services as they are currently provided are unlikely to satisfy disabled people and fall short of the demands made by disabled people from all over Europe when they met at a conference in Strasbourg to discuss their own struggles for independent living.

> We demand social welfare systems that include personal assistance services that are consumer controlled and which allow various models of independent living for disabled people, regardless of their disability and income. We demand social welfare legislation which recognises these services as basic civil rights and which provide necessary appeal procedures.
>
> (ENIL 1989)

The growing collective confidence of disabled people to demand appropriate welfare services as a civil right will be returned to subsequently. At present it remains true that welfare services are failing, and are likely to continue to fail to accord disabled people the entitlements of citizenship and, to return to the discussion at the end of the previous section, this failure for disabled people in general is compounded when discussing particular groups.

> It is not difficult to see the practical ways in which welfare mechanisms have failed to 'integrate' many sections of a differentiated 'collectivity' both formally and informally. The formal denial of welfare rights to women and to racialised groups both in the welfare legislation of the 'Great Liberal Reforms', through Beveridge to present day legislation, is well documented and the unofficial racism and sexism associated with the workings of welfare institutions is increasingly being exposed.
>
> (Taylor 1989, p. 25)

The argument so far could be summed up by saying that

the twin ideals of welfare citizenship and of rights were tentatively incorporated into the initial legislation which was to lay the foundations of the welfare state as we know it. However, everything that has happened since has been a retreat from these ideals whether it be in the dependency creating approaches to service provision, the interventionist nature of professional practice or the patronising language used to describe all this.

## Changing the context of community care

While therefore the current re-structuring is unlikely to transform disabled people into active citizens, it does raise the issue of whether the climate of change it has created offers disabled people a window of opportunity to enable them to transform themselves into active citizens.

There are two major forces shaping the changes that are occurring in the provision of community care. The first of those is the implications of the National Health Service and Community Care Act (1990) and the way statutory responsibilities are changing as a consequence of it. The second force is the growing demands of service users to have a voice in the way services are provided to meet their needs. These forces are interrelated for, as statutory authorities switch to become purchasers rather then sole providers of services, so users become more vociferous in their demands for a voice in these services, whoever they are purchased or provided by.

There is a great deal at stake in the context of changing trends in the way support provision is organised and financed; clearly, there is considerable potential for negotiating budget transfers with Local Authorities which would allow much larger numbers of users to control their own support arrangements. Further, the new Community Care legislation offers greater opportunities for user involvement in the planning and delivery of services. In fact, one commentator has claimed 'It's no longer a question of "is user involvement a good thing?". Users' organisations demand it. Legislation requires it'. (Beresford 1992.)

The forces shaping these changes are not going to go away and hence there is little point in arguing about whether they are a good thing or a bad thing. A much more sensible approach is to attempt to influence the changes that are occurring in ways that enable providers and purchasers to meet their statutory obligations and to protect the interests of service users.

However, all this should take place against the fact that users have been 'discovered'; by central and local government, by professionals and by university academics. Colonisation by such a veritable and worthy army may well produce benefits, but to whom, one might ask? One might ask the carers' movement, where it seems that lots of non-carers have made a good living talking and writing about the issue of caring over the past ten years, while, in the meantime, carers have carried on doing what they have always done in the same appalling material circumstances.

Thus, while there are things to avoid, there are also examples of developments that could be followed. One such scheme was instigated by the Greenwich Association of Disabled People in 1988. The basic aim was to enable more disabled people in Greenwich to live independently in the community by employing their own support workers (Oliver and Zarb 1992). This aim is consistent with current philosophy in Community Care practice (e.g. 'Caring for People') and, most importantly, with the demands of disabled people themselves – as expressed by their national and international representative bodies.

The United Nations World Programme of Action in one of its resolutions encapsulates both the wishes of disabled people and the rhetoric of current Government policy.

> Member states should encourage the provision of support services to enable disabled people to live as independently as possible in the community and in so doing should ensure that persons with a disability have the opportunity to develop and manage these services for themselves.
>
> (UN World Programme of Action)

Thus the moral and political case for giving disabled people the kinds of services they are demanding, is indisputable. It is not just the UN and organisations of disabled people who support this view. There is significant support, even amongst the Government and directors of social services departments (DIG 1993) for such initiatives. The problem remains as to how such support in principle is translated into everyday reality for disabled people ourselves.

The crucial factor in determining whether such services are ever likely to be provided revolves round their economic viability. The Greenwich scheme we evaluated (Oliver and Zarb 1992) indicates that at both the micro and the macro levels, providing disabled people with the kinds of services they are demanding is actually cheaper. And our findings were recently supported by a study published by the Policy Studies Institute, an independent research organisation.

> It is unlikely that local authorities could provide services which were cheaper than the arrangements made by disabled people themselves.
>
> (Lakey 1993, p. 23)

The Greenwich scheme, and other similar schemes, can and do, provide a valuable model of support provision for disabled people. Our work (Oliver and Zarb 1992) suggests that independent living schemes are not just morally desirable and professionally appropriate, but they also offer the possibility of providing more cost effective and efficient services through switching from the overproduction of welfare services that people don't want or need and the underproduction of those that they do, to a situation where the services that are produced and purchased by statutory providers are precisely the services that users want and need.

This assertion is not merely an act of faith but of economic necessity. Clearly society is no longer able, or prepared, to fund dependency creating services and the onus is on us all to develop services which facilitate independence. Recently the USA has embarked on an even more radical course than just attempting to restructure welfare services, through the passage of comprehensive anti-discrimination legislation (The Americans with Disabilities Act 1990). That the Act became law was more to do with the economic rationality underpinning it than any moral concerns.

> The ADA presents an opportunity to turn the corner on policies promoting welfare-like dependence and to develop instead supports for independence in the context of working, living and recreating in the mainstream. In this sense, implementing the ADA is an opportunity to contribute to an improved economy. When persons with disabilities give up public subsidies for jobs, they leave funds in the public coffers. When they become taxpayers, they contribute directly to public treasuries. When persons with disabilities become consumers in the marketplace, they strengthen the economy.
>
> (West 1992, p. 333)

Independent Living Schemes offer similar possibilities in less grandiose but no less important ways and should be developed rapidly as a major mechanism for developing new approaches to community care.

The current context offers real possibilities for developing the kinds of services that disabled people and other users want. If we fail to take this opportunity, it will only be because those who manage existing services are incompetent and unable to switch to the production of services that people want or need, or that the real purpose of the welfare state is to provide employment services for middle class professionals rather than those who really need them.

In any event, the combination of welfare state restructuring and the reintroduction of the idea of citizenship onto the political agenda at least offers disabled people the possibility of using them as part of their struggle for independence, empowerment and liberation. In the next chapter, we will consider one further aspect of the restructuring, the individualisation of need, and the likely effect of this on the struggles of disabled people.

# 5
# Social Policy and Welfare: From Needs to Rights

## Introduction

This chapter is a further consideration of the welfare state and an attempt to identify some of the reasons why it has failed disabled people among others. There is one further influence that is relevant to the discussions herein and that is my own commitment to collective welfare provision and my concern that within the political left, there has been a dearth in recent theorising about state welfare. As it is sometimes said in respect of religion that the devil has all the best tunes, in recent years it is the right that has had the best theories about welfare.

This situation has been partly resolved by the publication of Doyal and Gough's (1991) seminal work on human need. However, as I discuss in this chapter, I have major reservations about basing collective provision upon the identification of individual human need. I remain unconvinced in the final analysis that the contradiction therein is resolvable in respect of state provided welfare and so I begin to attempt to articulate what an alternative might look like.

## Why welfare dependency?

The evidence that disabled people experience severe economic deprivation and social disadvantage is overwhelming and no longer in dispute, whether it be from the Government's own commissioned research, from research institutes, academics or disabled people themselves. For example, after over a century of state-provided education disabled children and young people are still not entitled to the same kind of schooling as their able-bodied peers and nor do they leave with equivalent qualifications (Meltzer, Smyth and Robus 1989). The majority of British schools, colleges and universities remain unprepared to accommodate disabled students within a mainstream setting. Thus, many young disabled people have little choice but to accept a particular form of segregated 'special' education which is both educationally and socially divisive, and fails to provide them with the necessary skills for adult living. By producing educationally and socially disabled adults in this way, the special educational system perpetuates the misguided assumption that disabled people are somehow inadequate, and thus legitimates discrimination in all other areas of their lives.

Similarly, since the end of the Second World War at least, disabled people have consistently experienced higher rates of unemployment than the rest of the population, not because they are unable to work but because of the discriminatory behaviour of employers in failing to even attempt to meet their legal obligations under the quota system (Lonsdale 1986) and the lack of political will to insist upon its enforcement (Oliver 1985, a). As a result, currently, disabled people are more likely to be out of work than non-disabled people, they are out of work longer than other unemployed workers, and when they do find work it is more often than not low paid, low status work with poor working conditions (Martin, White and Meltzer 1989). This in turn accelerates the discriminatory spiral in which many disabled people find themselves.

The majority of disabled people and their families, therefore, are forced into depending on welfare benefits in order to survive (Martin and White 1988). Further, the present disability benefit system does not even cover impairment related costs and effectively discourages many of those who struggle for autonomy and financial independence. Dependence is the inevitable result and this is compounded by the present system of health and welfare services, most of which are dominated by the interests of the professionals who run them (Wolfensberger 1989; Oliver 1990; Davis 1990) and the traditional assumption that disabled people are incapable of running their own lives. Current welfare provision not only denies disabled people the opportunities to live autonomously but also denies them the dignity of independence within inter-personal relationships and the family home.

What is at issue is why this should be so, the role of welfare in compounding or alleviating this situation and what can be done about it. As I have already argued, the evidence that disabled people experience a quality of life so much poorer than everyone else is so overwhelming that it is not in dispute, though the precise dimensions of such deprivation and disadvantage may be (Disability Alliance 1990; Martin *et al.* 1989; Thompson *et al.* 1989).

At the level of theory, there can only be two possible explanations for this; one that disability has such a traumatic physical and psychological effect on individuals that they cannot ensure a reasonable quality of life for themselves by their own efforts; the other that the economic and social barriers that disabled people face are so pervasive that disabled people are prevented from ensuring themselves a reasonable quality of life by their own efforts.

The former has become known as the individual model of disability and is underpinned by personal tragedy theory. It has been under severe attack in recent years from a variety of sources to the point that it is now generally recognised that it is an inadequate basis for developing a proper understanding of disability. The latter has become known as the social model of disability and has shifted the focus away from impaired individuals and onto restrictive environments and disabling barriers. This has received acceptance to such an extent that it has almost become the new orthodoxy.

This chapter will not consider these issues any further as they have already been discussed in Chapter 3 in the context of individual and social models of disability. Instead I will examine the failure of the welfare state to ensure a decent life for disabled people.

Central to this failure, I will argue, has been the placing of the concept of need at the centre of welfare provision; notably the organisation and delivery of services. The fact that need remains central to welfare provision is illustrated by the following quote from a local needs audit project;

> Anyone concerned with reshaping Britain's welfare state for the 21st century must address the question of need. Whatever else a welfare system is about – and this is a subject of deepening controversy – it is surely about the collective provision of services and facilities to meet individual needs. Broadly speaking, decisions are taken to pool resources where it is thought to be impossible, inefficient or unfair for individuals to meet their own needs, and yet to be in the general interest for their needs to be met.
>
> (Percy-Smith and Sanderson 1992, p. 1)

This statement places need as central to both provision and practice and has been endorsed in the recent changes stemming from the National Health Service and Community Care Act (1990) where care management is defined as 'the process of tailoring services to individual needs' (SSI 1991, p. 7).

But need is not simply central to provision and practice in welfare, its centrality to theories of welfare has also been eloquently restated

> we believe that a coherent, rigorous theory of human need must be developed to resurrect an acceptable vision of social progress and to provide a credible alternative to the neo-liberalism and political conservatism which have caused serious harm to so many within the capitalist world. However, such a theory must be informed by mistakes – some terrible, some foolish – of welfare state paternalism, Stalinist collectivism and other political practices which have been premised on the existence of common needs. A credible and morally attractive theory of human need must draw upon both liberal and socialist thought.
>
> (Doyal and Gough 1991, p. 3)

Doyal and Gough go on to argue that all needs can ultimately be reduced to two basic ones:

> Since physical survival and personal autonomy are the pre-

conditions for any individual actions in any culture, they constitute the most basic human needs – those which must be satisfied to some degree before actors can effectively participate in their form of life to achieve any other valued goals.

(Doyal and Gough 1991, p. 54)

Not everyone writing from a theoretical perspective is as confident as Doyal and Gough appear to be that the idea of need is central to human welfare. Indeed, it has been argued that the concept of need is essential to social control by the State

it was 'need', rather than simply poverty, upon which the interventionist discourses of social policy came to settle. That is to say, 'need' expressed as a component of a normative discourse of social management. Whilst the twentieth century was to witness a great relativisation of concepts of poverty, the concept of need grew ever more obscure, more flexible, diverse and many faceted. Poverty seemed to provide the state with a single point of access into the lives of the poorest, whereas 'need' offered several points of access and many levels and dimensions as it reflected a far richer conception of the human experience.

(Squires 1990, p. 111)

While the debates about whether human needs are universal and whether they are essential to welfare provision are important, they will not be pursued further here. What is at issue in this chapter is the role that need has played in the provision of welfare services for disabled people since the end of the Second World War. In this discussion, I am critical of the notion that collective welfare provision can be provided on the basis of assessments of individual need; a position which both left wing theorists like Doyal and Gough and a plethora of right wing politicians appear to share.

## The welfare background

As I argued in the previous chapter, the project to establish a welfare state which would provide 'cradle to grave' security for all its members, has failed disabled people. This failure can be traced back almost to the foundations of the welfare state during the Second World War. Although different language might have been used at the time, the philosophy underpinning the Beveridge Report was that of active citizenship within a framework of entitlements. However, in translating this philosophy into practice, the welfare state created passive rather than active citizens (Ignatieff 1989) and nowhere is this more clearly illustrated than in terms of what happened to disabled people.

Indeed, the first Act of Parliament to treat disabled people as a single group was the Disabled Persons (Employment) Act 1944 which attempted to secure employment rights for disabled people (Topliss 1983). Further, the Education Act 1944, underpinned by an egalitarian ideology, specified that disabled children should be educated alongside their peers in primary and secondary education (Tomlinson 1981).

However, it was the concept of need, first introduced in 1946 in the Regulations concerning the Education Act which opened the way for the professional domination of welfare provision. Subsequently Section 29 of the National Assistance Act (1948) laid a duty on local authorities to 'arrange services' for people, not to enable them to meet their own needs. It also became clear that implementation of the Disabled Persons (Employment) Act was more concerned with the attitudes of employers than the rights of disabled people seeking employment (Lonsdale 1986). And the Education Act 1944 became the legal mechanism for the establishment of a huge infrastructure of segregated special education based around eleven medical categories.

The argument could be summed up by saying that the twin ideals of active citizenship and of rights were tentatively incorporated into the initial legislation which was to lay the foundations of the welfare state as we know it. However, everything that has happened since has been a retreat from these ideals whether it be in the dependency creating approaches to service provision, the interventionist nature of professional practice or the patronising language used to describe all this.

But to return to the argument, this unfortunate retreat from active to passive citizenship and from rights-based to needs-based welfare provision, has been masked since the late 1950s by the rhetoric and policy of community care. Since the late 1950s there has been a concerted attempt by successive governments to reduce the numbers of people living in segregated institutions of one kind or another. The shift towards community based services took a decisive turn in the early 1960s when the Government announced its intention to reduce the number of beds in mental hospitals by half. The rhetoric of community care continued to obscure the reality that for many previously incarcerated people, living in the community bestowed no more rights other than perhaps to starve, freeze or die alone.

By the late 1960s attempts were being made to rationalise the chaos that was the reality of community care and as far as disability services were concerned the Chronically Sick and Disabled Persons Act 1970 was to be the vehicle for this rationalisation. This was even heralded at one point by two non-disabled commentators as a 'Charter (of rights) for the disabled' (Topliss and Gould, 1981) but the reality was that it was merely an extension of the needs-based welfare provision of the National Assistance Act 1948 (Keeble, 1979). Evidence of this can be found in that the list of services provided under Section 2 was little more than the list of services to be provided under Section 29 of the National Assistance Act and provision of these services was still dependent upon the assessment of individual need.

The only two extra duties to be imposed on local authorities under the 1970 Act were the duty to compile a register and the duty to publicise services. The former produced little information of value (Knight and Warren 1978) and the latter was widely ignored (Oliver 1983). The services listed under Section 2 only needed to be provided where it was 'practical and reasonable' to do so, and for most local authorities it wasn't so they didn't (Cook and Mitchell 1982, Keep and Clarkson 1993). Hence the 1970 Act gave disabled people no new rights but re-emphasised needs based provision even if it proved ineffective in meeting needs however defined (Borsay 1986; Beardshaw 1988).

This is not to deny that there have been some benefits deriving from needs-based provision in that the majority of disabled people now have more access to relatively more services and, on the whole, are less likely to end up in a segregated institution of one kind or another (Barnes 1991). On the other hand the price for those services is usually acceptance of invasions of privacy by a veritable army of professionals and the acceptance of services that the state thinks you should have or is willing to pay for, rather than those that you know you need.

A further price to pay is often socialisation into dependency because those very services are provided for rather than with disabled people, because the special education system instills passivity and because the voluntary organisations continue to to promote negative images of disability, accentuated by recent media events such as Telethon and Children in Need (Oliver 1989b, 1990). Hence one study found that disabled young people 'appear to have been conditioned into accepting a devalued role as sick, pitiful and a burden of charity' (Hutchinson and Tennyson 1986, p. 33)

The 1980s have not seen a reversal of this general trend; despite the rhetoric of integration, community care and rights; neither the Education Act 1981 nor the Disabled Persons (Services, Consultation and Representation) Act 1986 has added substantially to the rights of disabled people nor addressed the reality of institutional discrimination which is part of our everyday lives.

Nor have the recent policy and service developments changed this because the concept of need is central to the current community care reforms in exactly the same way as it has been central to the development of the welfare state, almost since its inception at the end of the Second World War. And, just as placing this concept at the centre of provision has led to many of the past failings in state welfare, its centrality in the new reforms is almost certain to guarantee the continuing failure of community care policies.

As I have already argued, the reforms make needs led assessment the linchpin of service delivery; such assessment being formulated into a care plan. However, it is clear that need is not easy to define and hence assessment of need will not be as easy or non-problematic as the reforms assume, or hope it will be. Above all else, assessment of need is an exercise in power, as even the language we use to talk about the exercise shows (Hugman 1991). The professional assesses the need of the client or the user, as they have now come to be called. And various studies over the years show that clients are very unhappy about the way professional assessments of all kinds have distorted or denied their needs (Borsay 1986; Oliver *et al.* 1988; Morris 1989).

The new reforms do not change this balance of power at all even if it is now the care manager who assesses the needs of the service user. Users do now have rights to see and even contribute to their care plans, but they have no greater rights to service and still no access to legally enforceable grievance procedures. Although writing before the recent legislation the situation described by Cohen (1985) remains unchanged.

> much the same groups of experts are doing much the same business as usual. The basic rituals incorporated into the move to the mind – taking case histories, writing social enquiry reports, constructing files, organising case conferences – are still being enacted.
>
> (Cohen 1985, p. 152)

In the post 1990 world, the same people, albeit with different job titles and perhaps in plusher buildings, are doing the same things to disabled people although they may now be 'doing a needs-led assessment' or 'producing a care plan'.

Another fundamental problem with needs-led assessment, is that it is going to take place in the context of fixed budgets. A major criticism of the old system was that people's needs were made to fit both the kinds of provision and the amount of resources available. Of course, it can be argued that the purchaser/provider split will ensure that services are fitted to needs rather than the other way round because care managers will be buying rather than providing services. Further, they will have a legal duty to buy the majority of services in the private and voluntary sectors. And of course they will, but only within the twin constraints of their budgets and what the private and voluntary sectors are willing and able to provide.

So while we might be cynical about the new reforms on the grounds that need is very difficult, if not impossible to define in a non-contentious way, and that assessments are bound to be resource-led where budgets are fixed; perhaps we should put this cynicism to one side and see what happens. However the evidence available so far indicates that little general progress is being made (Ellis 1993; Hoyes *et al.* 1993) and that their impact on the lives of disabled people may be negative (Morris 1993a,b).

Well it would be possible to do that if all this did not seem so familiar. The Education Act 1981 had exactly the same assumptions underpinning it. Assessment of educational need was central, it would be codified into a written statement, exactly like the care plan, and the Education Authority would then have a duty to match provision to identified need. However, in implementation, needs led provision quickly becomes resource led when the act '... calls for the authority to determine the special provision that should be made for them' (Booth 1993, p. 136).

For years educational psychologists have complained that they are being forced to act unprofessionally in respect of their responsibilities under the Education Act 1981. Many have consistently complained that their employers have forced them to tailor their needs assessment to both resources and currently available provision rather than to individual assessments of need.

If we now had a system for meeting the special educational needs of children that worked, even moderately well, then we would have grounds for optimism with the community care reforms. Despite the fact that the Act recognised that the special needs of most children could be met in integrated settings, very little progress has been made in this direction, clearly demonstrating that special education continues to be resource and provision-led, rather than needs-led (Swann 1992).

Nor have statements containing written definitions of need helped parents to get the kind of schooling they want for their children. Numerous studies have shown widespread dissatisfaction with the way education authorities have carried out their responsibilities and indeed, it has been estimated that many of these authorities are in breach of their statutory duties under the Act (Goacher *et al.* 1988; CSIE 1991).

More than ten years after implementation therefore, we have a chaotic situation, recognised by various HMI reports and recently confirmed by damning reports produced by the Audit Commission (1992a, b). The Government itself has recognised this, issuing a consultation document and a new bill.

If placing need as central to special education reforms has lamentably failed, why then is the Government risking repeating this failure by placing need at the centre of the community care reforms? One factor in this continuation of needs-based welfare is that the concept of need has come to dominate the 'discourse' on welfare. The French philosopher Foucault (1973) suggests that the way we talk about the world and the way we experience it are inextricably linked – the names we give to things shapes our experience of them and our experience of things in the world influences the names we give to them.

This concept and its relationship to language has been described as follows;

> Discourse is about more than language. Discourse is about the interplay between language and social relationships, in which some groups are able to achieve dominance for their interests in the way in which the world is defined and acted upon. Such groups include not only dominant economic classes, but also men within patriarchy, and white people within the racism of colonial and post-colonial societies, as well as professionals in relation to service users. Language is a central aspect of discourse through which power is reproduced and communicated.
>
> (Hugman 1991, p. 37)

In linking language to politics through the notion of discourse, Ignatieff argues that the discourse of welfare provision which emphasises compassion, caring and altruism, is inappropriate when applied to citizenship for

> The language of citizenship is not properly about compassion at all, since compassion is a private virtue which cannot be legislated or enforced. The practice of citizenship is about ensuring everyone the entitlements necessary to the exercise of their liberty. As a political question, welfare is about rights, not caring, and the history of citizenship has been the struggle to make freedom real, not to tie us all in the leading strings of therapeutic good intentions.
>
> (Ignatieff 1989, p. 71)

Hence the linking of citizenship to welfare has unfortunate consequences because it has served to deny people their entitlements as citizens.

> The pell-mell retreat from the language of justice to the language of caring is perhaps the most worrying sign of the contemporary decadence of the language of citizenship ... Put another way, the history of citizenship of entitlement is a history of freedom, not primarily a history of compassion.
>
> (Ignatieff 1989, p. 72)

What this is drawing attention to is the inescapable fact that language and its use is not just a semantic issue; it is a political issue as well. And a political issue related to empowerment as well, in both the collective and personal sense of the term.

> The imposition of colonial languages on the natives, Oxford English on the regions, sexist language on women, racist language on black people, spoken language on deaf people, and so on, are all forms of cultural domination. Pidgin, dialects, slang, anti-sexist and anti-racist language and sign language are not, therefore, quaint and archaic forms of language use but forms of cultural resistance.
>
> (Oliver 1989, c.)

One final point needs to be made about the political function of language. It is not enough to realise that language is a political issue simply in an overt sense of the word. Politics as the exercise of power is sometimes as much about keeping things off the political agenda as it is about ensuring that they are debated (Lukes 1974).

Thus the point about language is that it may sometimes serve to obscure or mystify issues – even the language of rights as Hall graphically reminds us

> the language of rights is frequently deployed to obscure and mystify this fundamental basis which rights have in the struggle between contending social forces. It constantly abstracts rights from their real historical and social context, ascribes them a timeless universality, speaks of them as if they were 'given' rather than won and as if they were given once-and-for-all, rather than having to be constantly secured.
>
> (Hall 1979, p. 8)

It is for this reason that I took issue with the published history of Disabled Peoples International (Driedger 1988) which was entitled *The Last Civil Rights Movement*. Following Hall, there can never be a last such movement.

Given this proviso, it is nonetheless rights to appropriate welfare services to meet their own self-defined needs that disabled people are demanding, not to have their needs defined and met by others.

disabled people themselves are demanding a new emphasis on civil rights, equal opportunities and citizenship. They see institutional discrimination as the main disability they face, and are lobbying for new equal rights legislation to outlaw discrimination on the grounds of disability. The first priority is equal access to basic essentials such as an adequate income, housing, access to employment, to public transport, to education and to the ordinary facilities of everyday life.

(Doyle and Harding 1992, p. 72)

To return to an earlier debate, that of welfare services based upon the idea of citizenship rather than need. One commentator suggests that disabled people

were seeking a model of welfare built not on need and philanthropy, but on equal citizenship as a means of self determination'.

(Coote 1992, p. 5)

## Reconceptualising the problem: from needs to rights

Hence it is not denied any longer that the systematic deprivation and disadvantage that disabled people experience is caused by restrictive environments and disabling barriers. The point at issue here is what should be done about it. Up to now, successive governments have taken the view that the way to deal with this is through the provision of professional services aimed at meeting individual needs coupled with a strategy aimed at persuading the rest of society to remove their disabling barriers, and to change their restrictive environments. As a former Minister for Disabled People put it.

Nor would I deny that discrimination exists – of course it does. We have to battle against it, but, rather than legislating, the most constructive and productive way forward is through raising awareness in the community as a whole.

(Hansard 1991, 1150)

As I have already argued, professionalised service provision within a needs-based system of welfare has added to existing forms of discrimination and in addition, has created new forms of its own including the provision of stigmatised segregated services such as day care and the development of professional assessments and practices based upon invasions of privacy as well as creating a language of paternalism which can only enhance discriminatory practices.

On top of that, policies of persuasion have turned out to be bankrupt as the cost of implementing them grows while at the same time disabled children are still directed into segregated special schools, the numbers of disabled people who are unemployed increases, and the number of disabled people living in poverty continues to expand. That this unacceptable situation is due to disabling barriers rather than personal limitations is now clear; it is also clear that previous attempts to dismantle these barriers have been based on incorrect understandings of the real nature of discrimination. Discrimination does not exist in the prejudiced attitudes of individuals but in the institutionalised practices of society.

This new understanding of the real nature of the problem involves the idea of institutional discrimination which can be described in the following ways. Firstly, institutional discrimination is evident when the policies and activities of public or private organisations, social groups and all other organisational forms result in unequal treatment or unequal outcomes between disabled and non-disabled people. Secondly, institutional discrimination is embedded in the work of welfare institutions when they deny disabled people the right to live autonomously either through failure to meet their statutory obligations in terms of service provision, through their differential implementation of legislative and advisory codes, through interference in the privacy of disabled people or through the provision of inappropriate and segregative services (Barnes 1991).

## Conclusion

This chapter has argued that discrimination against disabled people is institutionalised throughout society and that welfare provision has compounded rather than alleviated that discrimination. The point needs to be made again that providing welfare services on the basis of individual need has failed disabled people. Because the needs of disabled people cannot be reduced to 'any conception of common human need', Doyal and Gough (1991, p. 322) would reject the arguments of this chapter as 'relativist'.

The fact remains that providing welfare services on the basis of individual need has aided the process of excluding disabled people from society rather than facilitated their inclusion. The dangers of exclusion have been starkly identified in a recent commentary on community care.

> Exclusion led to depersonalisation and a moral invisibility which were the necessary prelude to the organisation of the 'final solution'. That was made possible by the very nature of modern bureaucratic forms of organisation.
>
> (Wardhaugh and Wilding 1993, pp. 6–7)

Exclusion often begins with the education system which is the topic for the next chapter which will also discuss the switch in terminology from integration to inclusion. Subsequent chapters will come back to the links between exclusion and the 'final solution' for disabled people.

# 6
# Education for All? A Perspective on an Inclusive Society

## Introduction

One of the functions of welfare provision in general, and education in particular, is to ensure the integration of individuals into society. And, citizenship is a shorthand device for talking about the relationship between individuals and society. Then it is not surprising that the National Curriculum Council can affirm that the twin aims of education are to teach all children about the rights and responsibilities of citizenship.

> Education for citizenship embraces both responsibilities and rights in the present and preparation for citizenship in adult life. It helps pupils by supporting them as they develop from dependent children into independent young people. It is of paramount importance in a democratic society and in a world undergoing rapid change. . . . No school in England would

deny its responsibility for educating pupils for citizenship.

(NCC 1990, p. 1)

Unlike many of my disabled friends I do not have a personal interest in special education in that I did not go to special schools or colleges. I did however work for about ten years as a lecturer in special education, initially at a teacher training college and when we were 'absorbed' by the local polytechnic, within a faculty of education. My views on special education have been shaped both by the views of those who have been through the system, by the academic work I have read on the topic and by the contacts I have had over the years with schools, teachers and disabled children and their families.

It should not be assumed however, that my own personal experiences of disability have no relevance. When I moved from being a lecturer on disability to one on special education I was amazed at how similar the issues were and how similar were the experiences of users of special education to the experiences of users of other welfare services. All such services were, and still are, dominated by the professionals who produce them, were patronising and failed to offer disabled people choice or control in their lives. The rhetoric of the statement from the National Curriculum Council remains precisely that.

Over the years I have written various papers on the topic of special education (Oliver 1985, 1991b) and this builds on this work. In this chapter, I will argue that the education system has failed disabled children in that it has neither equipped them to exercise their rights as citizens nor to accept their responsibilities. Further, as I have already suggested, I will argue that the special education system has functioned to exclude disabled people not just from the education process but from mainstream social life. In order to understand why, we need to start with recent history.

## A recent history of special education

Undoubtedly the most important issue in respect of the education of disabled children over the last twenty years has been that of integration and this has overshadowed both the rhetoric and reality of debates about education for citizenship as far as disabled children are concerned. The Education Act of 1944, despite a philosophical commitment to the idea that disabled children should be educated, where possible, in ordinary schools, was the most important factor in the establishment of a large and complex system of segregated special education organised around a collection of eleven basically medical categories of disability (Tomlinson 1982).

Despite the humanitarian intentions underpinning the development of this segregated system of special education, by the 1960s it was becoming obvious that it was failing the vast majority of disabled children, both in educational terms and in terms of personal and social development. Consequently pressure was mounting on the Government to do something about the situation and it appointed a committee, to be chaired by Lady Warnock, to look into the matter. This began its deliberations in 1974 and published its influential report in 1978.

The Warnock Report and the Education Act of 1981 which stemmed directly from it both supported the principle of integration but the Act specified that there would be no extra money to make it happen and that it should not adversely affect the education of other children. While the Act gave parents some small additions to their rights, notably in terms of access to information, it added nothing to the rights and entitlements of citizenship for disabled children.

Certainly it did not provide access to the same educational facilities as other children and, in fact, since its passage the number of children educated in segregated special schools has hardly changed at all (Swann 1991). While the number of special schools has declined in absolute terms, this decline has been slower than the closure rate of ordinary schools consequent upon falling school rolls (Barnes 1991).

Thus, while the education of disabled children has been subject to major educational scrutiny and legislative change over the last twenty years, most disabled children are still being educated in special schools and still receive an education inferior to other children. A recent series of damning reports from HM Inspectors have criticised the accommodation and facilities provided and one report found that in only four of 36 special schools was access to specialist areas of the curriculum like science, satisfactory (for review of the evidence, see Barnes 1991, pp. 43–6).

The Warnock Report and the 1981 Act were almost the final product of the old welfare consensus as applied to education. The aim of the Government from the mid-1980s onwards has been to radically restructure the welfare state subjecting both the provision of services and the actions of professionals to the rigours of the market.

The Education Reform Act 1988 was to be the vehicle for bringing the discipline of the market into the process of schooling and the practice of teaching.

> The range of changes emanating from the implementation of the 1988 Education Reform Act are being driven and legitimated by a commitment to the importance of a market approach to educational provision and practice.
>
> > (Barton 1993, p. 35)

But, as was suggested in the context of the welfare market in the previous chapters, free markets cannot really be allowed to act with complete freedom (except in the barmier economic textbooks, of course). So in education, the Government introduced the national curriculum in order that schools and teachers can do what they like as long as, at the end of the day, the national curriculum is delivered.

Putting the curriculum in the centre of education has shifted the focus of the debate about the education of disabled children from issues of where it should take place to what it should be about. Additionally, the Government's pronouncement that the national curriculum was 'an entitlement curriculum' which applied to all pupils seemed to suggest that disabled children were going to be treated in exactly the same way as everyone else and be educated for citizenship.

The Act and subsequent regulations allow for the modification or disapplication of the national curriculum for disabled children in certain situations and under certain conditions at the discretion of the head teacher. And, as we have already suggested, the Government's own inspectorate have shown that curriculum delivery is inadequate in most special schools.

Precisely how modification and disapplication is operating remains hazy as the Act is only now being fully implemented. However, as the Act gives no new rights to disabled children and is unlikely to challenge the dependency creating tendencies of special schools, it seems likely that disabled children will still receive an inferior education to everyone else. Further, in being denied access to a curriculum to which everyone else is entitled, their educational opportunities will remain limited and their feelings of social inferiority will be reinforced. To have an entitlement to which you are not entitled is a clear denial of the rights of citizenship for disabled children. And one commentator has sounded a warning

> In this world of economic-led decision making, schools will find it difficult not to be involved in the divisive process of exclusion.
>
> (Barton 1993, p. 36)

## The integration/segregation debate revisited

While the 1988 Act may have shifted the focus of the educational debate somewhat; the arguments over the pros and cons of integration/segregation remain of central importance. What is interesting about this debate however, has been its narrowness, both in terms of its failure to see it as anything rather than a technical debate about the quality of educational provision. Its failure to explicitly develop any connections with the functional integration of individuals into society and its relationship to the citizenship rights and duties of disabled children, has been a major omission.

Accepting that disability is a human rights issue requires us to broaden our horizons in fundamental ways. To begin with, our current segregative practices and segregated provision, which continue to dominate the education of disabled children, have to be seen for what they are; the denial of rights to disabled people in just the same way as others are denied their rights in other parts of the world.

In a review of a recent re-appraisal of special education I wrote.

> The lessons of history through the segregation of black people in the United States and current struggles to end segregation in South Africa have shown this to be so. To write as if segregation in schools, or from public transport systems or from public spaces or inter-personal interactions in our own society is somehow different, is to de-politicise the whole issue.
>
> (Oliver 1991b)

What is both interesting and unfortunate about this debate in the area of education however, has been its narrowness, both in terms of its failure to see integration as anything other than a technical debate about the quality of educational provision. Its failure to explicitly develop any connections with other debates about segregation of, for example, disabled from public transportation systems, of black people in South Africa, of blind people from public information, or of the poor from major parts of our cities, has been a major omission.

An important reason for this is that integration, as a concept, has been taken over by politicians, policy makers, professionals and academics, who have discussed and debated it, divorced from the views of disabled people themselves. Even my own discipline of sociology, which has a justifiable reputation for criticising everything in sight including itself, has focused little on the exclusion of disabled people from society and its institutions (Oliver 1990).

While it is certainly true that in the early 1980s sociologists played a significant role in exposing the humanitarian ideology underpinning the segregation of children with special needs and exposing the various vested interests concerned (Tomlinson 1982; Ford *et al.* 1982), this was somehow seen in isolation from other exclusionary processes (Oliver 1985, b). Further, sociologists have spent less time examining and criticising the theory and practice of integration except for a questioning of the romanticism of the integration movement (Barton and Tomlinson 1984) and an articulation of its moral and political basis (Booth 1989).

In what follows, I shall attempt to expose the issue of integration, as it is currently understood and advocated, to a sociological critique and to advance a more appropriate sociological understanding of this issue. This critique will be based upon the attempts of disabled people (sociologists among them) to develop an understanding of the political and social contexts in which they live.

The issue of integration, both into society and into the education system, has been in the forefront of these attempts to develop such an understanding. However, precisely because integration as a concept has been taken over by politicians, policy makers and professionals, we have seen the emergence of two views of integration; what I shall call 'old' and 'new' views of integration. It should be obvious from Table 6.1 that it is the new views of integration that are emerging from disabled people themselves.

TABLE 6.1 *Integration*

| Old views | New views |
|---|---|
| 1. State | 1. Process |
| 2. Non-problematic | 2. Problematic |
| 3. Professional and administrative approaches | 3. Politics |
| 4. Changes in school organisation | 4. Changes in school ethos |
| 5. Teachers acquire skills | 5. Teachers acquire commitment |
| 6. Curriculum delivery must change | 6. Curriculum content must change |
| 7. Legal rights to integration | 7. Moral and political rights to integration |
| 8. Acceptance and tolerance of children with SEN | 8. Valuation and celebration of children with SEN |
| 9. Normality | 9. Difference |
| 10. Integration can be delivered | 10. Integration must be struggled for |

## A state or process

Almost since the beginning of discussions about the nature of integration it has been clear that integration is a complex and multi-faceted concept and not simply a matter of changing the place to which children were sent. Warnock (1978) distinguished between functional, locational and social integration and subsequent studies (Hegarty *et al.* 1981) argued that integration was not a new form of provision but a 'process geared to meeting a wider range of pupil needs'. Fish (1985) took this further and affirmed a commitment to the process of integration and spelled out in considerable detail the consequences of this view of integration for the whole education system and not just those limited parts that integration has previously been thought to reach.

While I do not disagree with any of this, our concern is that integration as process has taken on the language of rhetoric; to paraphrase Cohen (1985) quoted earlier, while the language has changed, the same groups of professionals are doing the same kinds of things to the same groups of children as they were before integration was ever mentioned. The rhetoric of integration has given rise to a new kind of educational discourse of which the changing labels of both professionals and children is a part. To put the matter bluntly, children with special educational needs still get an inferior education to everyone else, and although the rhetoric of integration as process may serve to obscure or mystify this fact, the reality remains. Hence

> Such simplified forms of discourse are essentially fraudulent. They misrepresent and thereby underestimate the seriousness of the issues involved and the degree of struggle required for the necessary changes to be realised. Thus they are, in and of themselves, part of the disabling process.
>
> (Barton and Corbett 1990, p. 9)

## Problematic or non-problematic

It is my contention, therefore, that the educational literature on integration sees the whole issue as non-problematic; integration has become received educational wisdom and can be paraphrased as follows: 'we know what integration is, we know that people want it and that we are all committed to it, so let's go ahead and do it'. This old view of integration has almost become the new educational orthodoxy and can preclude or, at least, make difficult the sociological function of critique. The concept of integration has become like the idea of motherhood – who can possibly be against it?

Integration has become re-ified; it has become an end in itself, not a means to an end. Not everyone is happy with this and, as in so many areas of life, this concern is initially expressed as a dissatisfaction with language. Hence the language of the debate is subtly shifting; from integration segregation to inclusion exclusion; and this shift is reflected in this chapter and the book more generally.

It is important to emphasise that I am not claiming that the struggle for integration is over except in an ideological sense. There is almost universal agreement that integration is a good thing given the right level of resources, the appropriate training of teachers and so on. The point that I am making is that the success of integration at an ideological level has made it almost impossible for it to be examined critically. Further, while sociology played an important role in the critique of segregation, it has not, as yet, provided a similar critique of integration.

By failing to be critical, sociology can never ask the right kind of questions of integration. Most importantly, how can integration be achieved in an unequal society? What are the consequences of integrating children into an education system which reflects and reinforces these inequalities? On the other hand, if integration is only the means to an end, what is that end and how might it be achieved? These, in my view, are the kinds of questions a new sociology of education must begin to ask in attempting to develop a new view of integration or inclusion, as it may become.

## Policy or politics

A non-problematic view of integration implies that the issue of successfully achieving integration is simply a matter of policy; a matter of framing the right legislation, of properly resourcing it and through regulation, ensuring that local authorities implement it properly. According to this view, integration has not yet been achieved despite commitments since Warnock (1978) and the Education Act (1981) for a number of reasons; government is not really committed to it and has not resourced it properly, it has been deliberately sabotaged by recalcitrant local authorities, professionals have used their power to prevent it, and educational administrators are too incompetent to ensure its implementation.

Whilst not disagreeing with the detail of this in my view the model of achieving social and educational change on which it is based is fundamentally flawed. At the end of the day, the kinds of changes needed to achieve the new view of integration are changes that can only be achieved through politics; through groups getting together and forcing change through the political system. To put the matter succinctly, integration is a political as well as an educational process (Oliver 1988). Further, political change does not just occur in parliament or town halls, it can occur in schools too and even, when necessary, on the streets.

## Changes in school organisation or ethos

The old views of integration suggest that schools must change in order to accommodate children with special needs (Dessent 1987). The kinds of changes necessary relate to the establishment of special needs departments (Jones and Southgate 1989), the provision of support services both internal and external to the school (Davies and Davies 1989), the development of whole school policies (Ramasut 1989) and the implementation of education authority wide integration policies (Moore and Morrison 1988). These organisational changes need to be planned in advance and properly resourced with a clear vision of the aims and objectives necessary to achieve integration.

Again, these things are undoubtedly necessary but, in themselves, they are not enough. There must also be changes in the ethos of the school which must mean that the school becomes a welcoming environment for children with special needs; that there is no questioning of their rights to be there and that organisational changes are part of an acceptance and understanding of the fact that the purpose of schools is to educate all children, not merely those who meet an increasingly narrowing band of selection criteria (ILEA 1985).

## Teachers acquire skills or commitment

As far as teachers are concerned it is usually assumed that they need to acquire extra knowledge and different skills in order to facilitate the process of integration. Changes in teacher education at both initial and in-service levels have tended to reinforce this (Sayer and Jones 1985). The problem is, of course, beyond the additions in knowledge and skills that any professional working in a new area would be expected to provide; it is hard to specify what this new knowledge or these new skills might be.

Hence the arguments advanced against integration until teachers have been properly trained can be seen as rationalisations to preserve the status quo rather than genuine concerns about the inabilities of teachers to cope with a whole range of new demands. In my view, teaching is teaching, regardless of the range or needs of pupils, and an essential prerequisite of integration in the new sense of the word is the acquisition of a commitment on the part of all teachers to work with all children, whether they have special needs or not. Only when teachers acquire this commitment can integration truly be achieved.

## Curriculum change – content or delivery

In terms of the curriculum, old views of integration suggest that it is delivery that must change. The Education Act (1988) and the introduction and implementation of a national curriculum have not done very much to change that. Underpinning this is the intention that children with special needs shall have access to exactly the same curriculum as everyone else and that curriculum delivery must change in order to ensure this access. Only in certain circumstances or under certain conditions will the national curriculum be disallowed.

The problem with this is that nowhere in the national curriculum is the issue of disability considered for any children, whether they have special needs or not. Despite controversy, it is generally acknowledged that curriculum materials have, up to now, been sexist or racist in their content. With one notable exception (Mason and Rieser 1990), there has been no acknowledgement that disablism actually exists, let alone admit the fact that the curriculum is full of disablist material from assessment procedures through children's fiction and onto assumptions about normal child development. Nothing short of the removal of all disablist curriculum materials will suffice if the new vision of integration, as we are coming to understand it, is ever to be achieved.

## Normality or difference

The old view of integration is underpinned by a notion of 'normality' and preaches the acceptance and tolerance of children with special needs. People, teachers and children, need to be encouraged and sometimes educated to this acceptance and tolerance of those who deviate from normality. Hence disability awareness training becomes a major mechanism for this education and the aim of a whole variety of policies and programmes in many different spheres, is to promote this public education.

The new view of integration challenges the very notion of normality in education (Oliver 1989a) and in society generally (Abberley 1989) and argues that it does not exist. Normality is a construct imposed on a reality where there is only difference. Disability equality training, pioneered, developed and run by disabled people themselves (Campbell and Gillespie-Sells 1991) is becoming the major means for ensuring that integration based upon difference becomes a politically achievable reality.

## Acceptance and tolerance or valuation and celebration

The old view of integration suggests that these people who are different have to be accepted and tolerated for after all, the different have come to accept and tolerate their difference so why shouldn't everyone else. This view is underpinned by personal tragedy theory in terms of disability and deficit theory in educational terms. Tragedies and deficits are unfortunate, chance happenings and these poor individuals should not be made to suffer further through rejection and stigmatisation; hence they should be accepted and tolerated.

The new view of integration is underpinned by an entirely different philosophy, what might be called the politics of personal identity. This demands, and has the confidence to demand it through a growing collective identity, that difference not be merely tolerated and accepted but that it is positively valued and celebrated. Further, in making these demands, it is not just a matter of providing a legal framework but backing that framework with moral fervour and political will to ensure its enforcement.

## Legal or moral and political rights to integration

The thorny issue of rights is one that has bedeviled attempts at integration, not just in the narrow sphere of education nor only in Great Britain. In Britain legislation, at least since 1944, has endorsed the principle and philosophy of integration but has insisted that it could only take place where practical and reasonable, where it did not interfere with the education of other children or where it was commensurate with existing resources. Such let out clauses, for that is what they are, have meant that integration has not taken place.

What is needed, according to the new view of integration, is a moral commitment to the integration of all children into a single education system as part of a wider commitment to the integration of all disabled people into society. Translating this moral commitment into political rights is something that can only be achieved by supporting disabled people and the parents of children with special needs as they struggle to empower themselves. Support for these struggles may stem from a moral commitment but it must be properly resourced struggles in terms of both money and other services.

## Integration – delivery or struggle

What is at stake in this dispute between old and new views of integration is nothing less than our view of both the nature of social reality and the role of politics in society. The old view sees integration as a humanitarian response to unintended consequences in our past history which can be changed by the development of paternalistic policies. The new view suggests that

> Integration is not a thing that can be delivered by politicians, policy makers or educators, but a process of struggle that has to be joined.
>
> (Oliver 1991, b, 143)

And in recognition of that, it is perhaps time we renamed that struggle as inclusion.

## Education for citizenship

Given that the struggle for inclusion is also part of the struggle for citizenship, and that this struggle has to be broadened beyond the narrow realm of education, then the relationship of education to the economy needs to be considered. For too long education in all sectors has colluded with the demands of the labour market to keep disabled people out of the workforce. Most disabled children leave school thinking they are unemployable and immediately have this reinforced by social education centres and colleges of further education with their offers of 'further on' courses and 'independence training'.

All part of a collusion given respectability by the Warnock Report and its endorsement of 'significant living without work'. Even higher education, with its recent 'discovery' of the disabled student, is happy to keep disabled people out of the labour market for as long as the economic benefits accrue to them.

So disabled school leavers may have a range of choices; from the day centre to the FE or HE establishment and so on. But very few will have their rights as citizens to enter the labour market, with a reasonable chance of getting a job, realised. Hence, they will continue to be denied the opportunities to exercise their duties and responsibilities as citizens. This is not because disabled people are unable to work, though the special education system may socialise them into believing the opposite; it is because of the way in which the labour market operates (Oliver 1991a; Berthoud *et al.* 1993; Lunt and Thorton 1994).

To understand why this is so, it is necessary to go back to the Second World War. As able-bodied men were called up, the consequent labour shortages were solved by the recruitment of women and disabled people into all sectors of the economy. Between 1941 and 1945 426 000 disabled men and women – many of whom were classified as unemployable – were interviewed by officials from the labour exchanges. Of those 310 806 were placed in full-time employment.

Two historians, in a book which accompanied a Channel 4 series on the history of disability, comment thus.

> Disabled people were integrated into the workforce, working alongside the able-bodied. In some factories the hearing learned sign language to communicate with deaf workers. And more and more disabled people were given skilled and responsible jobs. In all around half a million disabled people were recruited into full time employment during the war.... *It was all part of a new recognition of their economic importance at a time when their labour power was desperately needed.* [My emphasis]

> (Humphreys and Gordon 1992)

In the intervening period, the labour power of disabled people has not changed although the labour market's need of it obviously has. Hence, only a third of disabled people of working age are in employment. Of course, I fully realise that education cannot control the labour market overall, but it can and does collude with it and it fails to exercise its responsibilities in those parts of the labour market it does control.

It colludes by socialising disabled people into accepting a life without work and by failing to give disabled people the necessary skills to enter into the labour market in the first place. It fails to exercise its responsibilities by its employment practices;

education as an employer is no better at employing disabled people than any other sector of the economy.

A human rights perspective on these issues does not mean that disabled people should have a right to a job; rather that disabled people should have an equal chance of unemployment as everyone else. This means giving disabled people the skills and values to compete in the labour market with everyone else and ensuring that the market, or that bit of the market over which control can be exerted, operates in such a way it does not discriminate against them. On both these accounts, education has failed disabled people.

## Conclusion: towards a new understanding; inclusion instead of integration

The rediscovery of citizenship in the late twentieth century has not, however resulted in a greater understanding of the processes which exclude some groups from the mainstream of social life nor has it added substantially to their legal rights to be included. This lack of understanding extends, as I argued previously, to what integration actually means. The following quote demonstrates the point;

> If by integration you understand a breakthrough into able bodied society by disabled people, an assimilation and acceptance of disabled people into an already established set of norms and code of behaviour set up by the able bodied, then YES I am against it. . . . If on the other hand by integration you mean there shall be participation by all members of a society, catering for the full expression of the self in a freely changing society as determined by people, then I am with you.

I have deliberately not referenced this quote because it did not come from a disabled person; in fact, my attention was originally drawn to the quote by Bob Finlay many years ago, and I adapted it from the words of someone else, now properly reproduced.

> If by integration you understand a breakthrough into white society by blacks, an assimilation and acceptance of blacks into an already established set of norms and code of behav-

iour set up by whites, then YES I am against it.... If on the other hand by integration you mean there shall be participation by all members of a society, catering for the full expression of the self in a freely changing society as determined by people, then I am with you.

(Steve Biko, *I Write What I Like*,
Penguin Books, London, 1978, p. 38)

It is worth noting that special, segregated education has been the main vehicle for educating disabled children throughout most of the industrialised world in the twentieth century and in Britain since 1890. In that hundred years, the special education system has failed to provide disabled children with the knowledge and skills to take their rightful place in the world; to use a current buzz word, it has failed to empower them. According to one disabled American activist.

The business of society is empowerment. The legitimate purpose of human rights, of human society and its governments, is not simply to guarantee equal opportunity to pursue the good life. The purpose, the absolute responsibility of society is to empower all of its members actually to produce and to live the good life.

(Justin Dart)

This failure to empower is not something that will be tolerated in the twenty-first century. Disabled people, all over the world, are struggling to confront the processes that exclude and segregate them and to escape from the institutions that are part of that. The power of that struggle is captured in the following quote.

Increasingly we disabled people are raising our voices to speak against warehousing of disabled people in special institutions and against the denial of basic equal and civil rights. We no longer accept segregation and paternalization of disabled people by medical experts, policy makers and administrative officials.

(ENIL 1989)

The history of the twentieth century for disabled people has been one of exclusion. The twenty-first century will see the struggle of disabled people for inclusion go from strength to strength. In such a struggle, special, segregated education has no role to play.

The next chapter switches the focus to rehabilitation, but retains some continuity with this one in that the ideology of normality which underpins the process of education also underpins the rehabilitation enterprise.

# 7
# Rehabilitating Society

In the universities, both new and old, staff awarded the title of 'Professor' are required to provide an open lecture. This is often no easy task because not only are colleagues likely to turn up but also possibly clerical and secretarial staff as well as friends, family and the like. In my case this was certainly true and it is no easy task to give a lecture to such a diverse audience.

Such lectures are no easy task for the audience either for they risk being patronised, mystified or simply bored. The difficulties faced by my audience were compounded by the presence of a television crew who wanted background footage for a programme they were making and who proceeded as if the event had been staged entirely for their benefit and then added insult to injury by not showing a single foot of the film they shot. It was, perhaps fortunate that I had produced the lecture as text otherwise chaos might have resulted. It is this text that is produced below.

## Introduction

It is, perhaps, perverse to choose as the focus for my professorial lecture, an activity that I myself have not engaged in for more than thirty years. It may be, but it is also deliberate. It is to counter the criticism sometimes wrongly levelled at my work; namely that I regard personal experience as more important than methodology. In other words, I believe that only disabled people should do disability research.

To say that research by able-bodied researchers has served disabled people badly, or indeed work by men has served women badly and work by whites has served black people badly, is not privileging experience over methodology. It is criticising inaccurate, distorting and at times, downright oppressive, sociological research dominated by white, able-bodied males. Hence, I hope to demonstrate that a non-walker can make a significant contribution to our understanding of walking, both sociologically and anthropologically and without distorting the experience of walkers.

Before going on to develop this further, I should include a cautionary note about the political correctness of the terminology I shall be using. I am well aware that disabled people is the politically correct term for describing the people I will be discussing, but I am going to put that aside for the purposes of this lecture. As walking is the central, organising concept of the discussion, I am going to divide the world into walkers, non-walkers and nearly-walkers.

When I have finished may be the time to discuss the political correctness or incorrectness of this classification but if I offend any disabled people, then I apologise in advance. If I offend any academics, researchers or professionals who have wrongly categorised us or distorted our experience with their schemes; then now you know how it feels.

Finally, I should add that walking is an appropriate topic for my professorial lecture, for as a young academic, the very first paper I ever had published was on this subject; in the *International Journal of Medical Engineering and Technology*. For a sociologist this was no small feat. Having re-read this paper recently when preparing this lecture, I was pleasantly surprised to find how much I still agreed with. So much so that I was tempted merely to reproduce it as the lecture and then confess at the end.

However, while that might have been a clever trick, it would not have shown how my own understanding of walking has developed over the years and the role that sociology has played in this development. So, for those of you bursting to know how clever and insightful I was all those years ago, you will have to be satisfied with the following quote unless you want to read the original yourself.

> the aim of research should not be to make the legless normal, whatever that may mean, but to create a social environment where to be legless is irrelevant.
>
> (Oliver 1978, p. 137)

While I cringe, some fifteen years later, at the political *incorrectness* of some of my terminology, I still agree with the sentiment behind it.

I would not want to pretend that, following such seminal insights, such a thing as the sociology of walking has sprung up or even that sociologists have been queuing up to study the topic in the way that they have other more sexy topics like class, or deviance, or medicine, or more recent discoveries like race and gender. However the sociology of the body has become sexy recently and one of its leading theorists, Bryan S. Turner, made a throw-away comment on walking in one of his attempts to theorise the body. He wrote,

> Walking is a capacity of the biological organism, but it is also a human creation and it can be elaborated to include the 'goose-step', the 'march', and 'about-turn'. Walking is rule-following behaviour, but we can know a particular person by his walk or by the absence of a walk. . . . . my way of walking may be as much a part of my identity as my mode of speech. Indeed, the 'walk' is a system of signs so that the stillness of the migrainous person or the limp of the gouty individual is a communication.
>
> (Turner 1984, p. 236)

What for him was a throw-away comment, I take as the starting point for this lecture. Walking is not merely a physical activity which enables individuals to get from place A to place B. It is also a symbolic act, but not merely symbolic as far as individuals are concerned; it is also culturally symbolic and therefore it is necessary to understand walking sociologically, given that a central problematic of sociology is to understand 'the meaning of life'.

I do not intend here to provide 'the' or even 'a' sociology of walking, nor do I intend to sketch out an agenda for what a sociology of walking might look like. Instead, I shall apply some sociological ideas to the issue of walking and see how far that gets us. In so doing, I shall focus on three areas; the meaning of walking at the cultural level; the pursuit of the idea of walking as a millenarian rather than medical activity; and the influence of the ideology of walking on the enterprise of rehabilitation. Finally, I shall address some remarks to the purpose of this, or, to quote the words of a currently unfashionable sociologist called Lenin, 'What is to be done?'

## Walking and culture

In considering the meaning of walking at the cultural level, I have decided to concentrate on its cultural production within the realms of the popular song, not simply because it is something I have a passing interest in, but because popular songs tell us more about the meaning of life than do other more elitist cultural forms such as squawking in a foreign language, jumping around on stage by over-muscled men and anorexic women or reading Sunday supplement novels.

My interest in the relationship between popular song and walking was awakened by a remark made by David Swift, a nearly-walker who appeared on the recent Channel 4 series on the history of disability. As a nearly-walker, he was reflecting on his ability or inability to attract girls in the dance halls of Nottingham in the 1950s:

> I didn't have many girlfriends, more casual acquaintances. Once they got to know the way I walked ... I mean there were plenty of songs coming out where they say, 'Look at the way she walks'. Everything was 'He walks like an angel ... Just walking in the rain ... Walking my baby back home'. And I'm thinking to myself about all these songs related to walking. And I couldn't even walk properly. What had I got to show? But I found the key pretty early. I found the key to getting a girl was to play the fool. I'd got to get their eyes away from my legs. So as long as I could keep them

laughing I was alright. But as soon as I saw their eyes lowering, I knew the danger was coming.

(Humphreys and Gordon 1992, p. 114)

Perhaps the song that says it all is one by Val Doonican called 'Walk Tall' which contains the refrain,

> Walk tall, walk straight
> and look the world right in the eye
> that's what my momma told me
> when I was about knee high.
> She said, son be a proud man
> and hold your head up high
> walk tall, walk straight
> and look the world right in the eye.

Though I don't know for sure, I like to think that when Lois Keith made her poetic attack on the sexist and ambulist nature of language, she had that song in mind. For those of you who don't know it, I'll include her poem here.

> Tomorrow I am going to re-write the English language
> I will discard all those striving ambulist metaphors
> Of power and success
> And construct new images to describe my strength
> My new, different strength.
> Then I won't have to feel dependent
> Because I can't stand on my own two feet
> And I will refuse to feel a failure
> When I don't stay one step ahead.
> I won't feel inadequate if I can't
> Stand up for myself
> Or illogical when I don't
> Take it one step at a time.
>
> I will make them understand that it is a very male way
> To describe the world
> All this walking tall
> And making great strides.
>
> Yes, tomorrow I am going to re-write the English Language,
> Creating the world in my own image.

Mine will be a gentler, more womanly way
To describe my progress.
I will wheel, cover and encircle
Somehow I will learn to say it all.

(Keith 1994, p. 57)

Popular songs do not simply dismiss non-walkers or nearly-walkers in symbolic or metaphorical terms. The classic of the genre is the Kenny Rogers hit which features the paralysed veteran of some 'crazy, Asian war' pleading with his wife not 'to take her love to town'. It contains my favourite lyric in the whole of popular music, 'It's hard to love a man whose legs are bent and paralysed.' So, non-walkers and nearly-walkers are not simply socially inadequate, they are sexually incompetent as well.

I know, just as one swallow doesn't make a summer, a few lyrics from one cultural form are not the whole story, but as more and more disabled people are subjecting other cultural forms to critical analysis, the full picture of just how disablist our culture really is, is beginning to emerge. But to stay unapologetically within the cultural form I have chosen, as Lesley Gore once sang, 'It's my party and I'll cry if I want to' so 'It's my lecture and I'll say what I want to'.

## Walking and cure

The pursuit of restoring the ability to walk or nearly walk is better understood, I would argue, as a millenarian movement rather than as the logical application of modern medical knowledge. For those of you unclear what such a movement is, I offer the following definition.

> In sociology, a millenarian movement is a collective, this-worldly movement promising total social change by miraculous means.
>
> (Abercrombie *et al.* 1988, 157)

In Britain, I would argue, a number of such movements currently exist exclusively, or almost exclusively, to solve the 'problem' of non-walking or nearly walking. They call themselves charities and they raise and spend probably in excess of one hundred million pounds in pursuit of cures for what they usually call 'chronic or crippling diseases' every year.

It could, and usually is, argued that these are organisations devoted to the pursuit of scientific research, and they cannot even be conceived of as millenarian movements awaiting the second coming, the arrival of the inter-galactic spaceships, the return of long-dead ancestors and the like.

The problem is, of course, that throughout the history of humankind, the number of cures that have been found to these 'chronic and crippling diseases' could be counted on the fingers of one hand and still leave some over to eat your dinner with. And in empirical terms, there are considerably more examples of 'so-called' miraculous cures, than there are of those produced by scientific medicine. Finally, creating a society where all non-walkers and nearly-walkers walked properly, would indeed require total social change.

Imagine it, Architects could let their imaginations run riot and design buildings without worrying about access; employers could recruit whoever they wanted without considering disabled applicants; the integration of disabled children would disappear; and all those professionals currently employed in 'looking after' disabled people would be out of work. Revolutionary social change indeed!

If we take one example with which I am familiar and in which I have a personal interest, then perhaps it will become even clearer. The example is the International Spinal Research Trust and an anthropological case study of it might look like the following:

A prophet wandered the land (Britain) and he had a vision; that all those who had a spinal injury would one day be able to walk again. Not only that but this could be achieved within five years if certain things were done. These included a range of behaviours and rituals and necessitated forming an organisation to support them. He wandered the land and spoke to people of both high and low status, those afflicted and those not and convinced some that his vision was true. So the organisation was formed.

But this was the beginning, not the end. In order for his vision to be achieved a number of rituals had to be performed and repeated. These included persuading the great and the good to get dressed in their finest clothes, go to places of high social status, drink too much alcohol, jump up and down and throw money at a table strategically placed at the end of the room. Those of lower social status performed rituals of a different kind; usually involving cutting holes in the tops of tins and then accosting non believers in the street and demanding that they place money in them. Even the afflicted were expected to participate, either by inviting people to their houses, offering them coffee and then charging them extortionate prices for it or by pushing their wheelchairs right round the island to end up in exactly the same place they had started from.

This was not the end of the rituals however, for the organisation then collected all this money and passed it on to a group of men of special status, who wore white coats and who worked in places called laboratories. These men, then proceeded to buy or breed thousands of animals who were then ritually slaughtered. These men in white coats then meticulously recorded these activities and wrote about them for other men in white coats who could not be present while the rituals were being performed.

However, despite religiously following these rituals for the appointed time period, the vision did not materialise in the time period specified, the original prophet was forced to flee the land to an island on the other side of the world (Australia). Whether he is still having visions is unknown. The sect did not however disintegrate at this point, but continues today, still urging its believers to intensify their rituals and indeed blaming them for the 'failure of prophecy'.

In case you think that my description is (too) subjective, which of course it is, as is all anthropology and, indeed, sociology, I here reproduce a statement from the current research director of the movement, responding to criticisms of their claims made by another organisation representing people with a spinal injury; the Spinal Injuries Association (SIA).

The criticisms in the SIA magazine were against a claim made in 1986 that a cure was realisable within 5 years. Given that this claim was hedged with the proviso that enough money had to be available, I still claim that it was not irresponsible . . . I still believe that the timing is not impossible. There can be no certainty that a model of cure can be constructed in the laboratory by the end of 1992, but progress on the repair of damaged tracts has been so swift that it should not be ruled out.

(Banyard 1991)

This quote contains all the elements that characterise the response of millenarian movements when prophecy fails. Firstly, the timeframe was elastic, not absolute. Secondly, the message was misunderstood; it was not a cure that was promised but 'a model of cure in the laboratory'. Thirdly, the rituals necessary to bring about the millennium were not properly followed; in this case, not enough money was raised.

It is not just nineteenth-century millenarian movements like the Melanese cargo cults or the North American Indian Ghost Dance, that these charities have much in common with, but also twentieth-century religious sects. One such sect visited Britain last year (1993) and claimed that 'some will be moved by the power of God for the first time'. And when, of course, no-one left their wheelchair and started to walk, it was because the message was misunderstood; people would be moved spiritually, not physically.

From the false prophets of religious evangelism, from the dashed hopes of cargo cultists, from the abandoned visions of the ghost dancers to the exaggerated claims of the impairment charities (Hevey 1992); the idea of restoring the function of walking to those who cannot or have lost the ability to do it, reigns supreme. It reigns supreme too, in the enterprise of rehabilitation.

## Walking and rehabilitation

Rehabilitation can be defined in many ways but what is certain is a whole range of practices stem from the definition adopted; to paraphrase the old W. I. Thomas dictum, 'if people define situations as real, then they are real in their consequences'. This is not contentious but the central problem with rehabilitation is that none of the definitions adopted can be shown to be in accord with the experience of disability and none of the practices stemming from these definitions can be shown to work effectively. To put matters bluntly, all is not well in the enterprise of rehabilitation, whether it be rehabilitation professionals expressing their anxiety (RCP 1986) or their victims, and I use the term advisedly, expressing their discontent (Oliver *et al.* 1988; Beardshaw 1988).

I shall argue that central to the problem of rehabilitation is the failure to address the issue of power and to acknowledge the existence of ideology; both good, reputable sociological concerns. Hence for me, rehabilitation is the exercise of power by one group over another and further, that exercise of power is shaped by ideology. The exercise of power involves the identification and pursuit of goals chosen by the powerful and these goals are shaped by an ideology of normality which, like most ideologies, goes unrecognised, often by professionals and their victims alike.

More of this later but let me further emphasise here that I am not suggesting that we can eradicate the influence and effects of power and ideology in rehabilitation, but that our failure to even acknowledge their existence gives rise to a set of social relations and a range of therapeutic practices that are disabling for all concerned, whether they be professionals employed in the provision of rehabilitation services or disabled people as recipients of these services.

Space will not permit a detailed, sustained and comprehensive critique of rehabilitation, so in order to illustrate my argument I shall focus on a topic at the heart of the rehabilitation enterprise and this lecture – that of walking.

Rehabilitation constructs the concept of walking uncritically in that it is never analysed or discussed except in technical terms – what surgical operations can we perform, what aids can we provide and what practices can we use to restore the function of walking? Walking is more complex and complicated than that, both as a physical act and, indeed, a social symbol, as I hope I have already demonstrated.

In terms set by the rehabilitation enterprise, walking is rule-following behaviour; not-walking is rule-ignoring, rule-flouting or even rule-threatening behaviour. Not-walking can be tolerated when individuals are prepared to undergo rehabilitation in order to nearly walk or to come to terms with their non-walking. Not-walking or rejecting nearly-walking as a personal choice is something different however; it threatens the power of professionals, it exposes the ideology of normality and it challenges the whole rehabilitation enterprise.

A classic example of the way the ideology of normality linked to an uncritical concept of walking informs rehabilitation practice is this description and analysis by a person with a spinal injury.

The aim of returning the individual to normality is the central foundation stone upon which the whole rehabilitation machine is constructed. If, as happened to me following my spinal injury, the disability cannot be cured, normative assumptions are not abandoned. On the contrary, they are reformulated so that they not only dominate the treatment phase searching for a cure but also totally colour the helper's perception of the rest of that person's life. The rehabilitation aim becomes to assist the individual to be as 'normal as possible'.

The result, for me, was endless soul-destroying hours at Stoke Mandeville Hospital trying to approximate to able-bodied standards by 'walking' with callipers and crutches.

(Finkelstein 1988, 4–5)

Nor indeed would I want to argue that most rehabilitation victims reject the idea of walking. One disabled person who clearly didn't was Philip Olds, an ex-policeman who was shot while trying to prevent an armed robbery. According to Jenny Morris,

As he put it, before his injury, 'I was a motorcycle riding, fornicating, beat walking, criminal catching man – a bit of a cross between Telly Savalas and Dennis Waterman'.

(Morris 1992, p. 2)

He couldn't accept not-walking or nearly walking and encouraged by both national newspapers and television producers, he pursued the idea of walking with a commitment bordering on desperation. As the general public, we read about and watched his efforts to walk, or nearly walk, with baited breath. He failed. While Vic Finkelstein, the author of the first quote, is still around more than thirty years after rejecting nearly-walking, Philip Olds took an overdose in 1986. One commentator said he had been 'pressed to death' (Davis 1987).

Polarising two such different examples is, of course, being selective but all attempts to understand the meaning of life depend upon us selecting and interpreting. I do not claim that my interpretation is the only one but I do claim that it is a valid one, and I further claim that it says much about the way power operates in the rehabilitation enterprise as well as much about the way the mass media operates currently.

Power, of course, is a slippery concept to define, let alone recognise in operation. According to Lukes (1974), central to the operation of power in society is what is not placed on the political (with a small p) agenda. Hence, as I have already suggested, the questions that are not asked are as important for rehabilitation as are those that are. A central question that is never asked of rehabilitation is its links with social control.

Questions concerning the therapeutic nature and effectiveness of rehabilitation are often asked; questions concerning the way rehabilitation often forces impaired individuals to do things that they would not freely choose to do for themselves are almost never asked. Links between the whole rehabilitation enterprise and wider aspects of social control are also never asked; after all, the ideology of the therapeutic state is caring, not controlling.

There are two dimensions to the operation of power which are relevant to questions of control; power to control the individual body and power to control the social body. The connections between the two are encapsulated in the work of the French philosopher Michael Foucault, whose discussion of health care systems has been summarised as follows;

> An essential component of the technologies of normalisation is the key role they play in the systematic creation, classification and control of anomalies in the social body.
>
> (Rabinow 1984, p. 21)

The relevance of the work of a dead French philosopher to rehabilitation may not be immediately apparent but if for 'technologies of normalisation', we read rehabilitation practices, then uncomfortable questions are raised. The quote might then look something like this.

> An essential component of the *rehabilitation enterprise* is the key role it plays in the systematic creation, classification and control of anomalies in the social body.

To put the point succinctly in the language of this lecture, the aim of rehabilitation is to encourage walking and nearly-walking, and to control through therapeutic interventions, non-walkers and nearly-walkers both individually and as a group.

Like power, ideology is at its most influential when it is invisible and the ideology of normality permeates throughout the whole of society; a society which, according to well known disabled actor Nabil Shaban, is based on body fascism. And of course, body fascism affects the lives of more of us than merely non-walkers and nearly-walkers; women for example to name one not unimportant section of the population.

The ideology of normality permeates most rehabilitation practice; from paediatrics through rheumatology and onto geriatrics. One example of where it surfaces is the current 'success' of conductive education. Many disabled people are profoundly disturbed by the ideology underpinning conductive education which I have likened to the ideology of Nazism (Oliver 1989a).

Lest anyone should be unclear about what's wrong with conductive education, its pursuit of nearly-walking to the detriment of family, social and community life for many disabled children, can only be countenanced as therapeutic intervention.

If able-bodied children were taken from their local school, sent to a foreign country, forced to undertake physical exercise for all their waking hours to the neglect of their academic education and social development, we would regard it as unacceptable and the children concerned would rapidly come to the attention of the child protection mafia. But in the lives of disabled children (and adults too), anything goes as long as you call it therapeutic.

What can be pernicious about ideology is not simply that it enables these issues to be ignored but sometimes it turns them on their heads. Hence conductive education is not regarded as child abuse but as something meriting social applause, as something to make laudatory television programmes about, as something worthy of royal patronage, and finally as something that should be funded by government and big business alike.

The reality, not the ideology of conductive education, and indeed many other rehabilitation practices, is that they are oppressive to disabled people and an abuse of their human rights. We should not pretend it is any other way.

This critique should not be regarded as an attempt to throw out the baby as well as the bath water. Rather it is an attempt to force onto the agenda of the rehabilitation enterprise, issues it has barely considered. It is my belief that properly addressing these issues will make rehabilitation a more appropriate enterprise for all concerned – not only will the bath water be clearer but the baby healthier as well. At the end of the day 'To "rehabilitate" rehabilitation (and other human service agencies), we need to "rehabilitate" ourselves' (Higgins 1985, p. 221).

## What is to be done

A similar point is made by Ken Davis when he says, 'We can elevate the act of walking to an importance higher than engaging in the struggle to create a decent society.' (Davis 1986, p. 4) The point is, as I hope I have demonstrated, that walking has a significance beyond merely the functional. If it did not have, why would society punish non-walkers for not walking?

After all, we do not punish non-flyers for not flying. In fact we do exactly the opposite. We spend billions of dollars, yen, deutschmarks and pounds every year providing non-flyers with the most sophisticated mobility aids imaginable. They are called aeroplanes. An aeroplane is a mobility aid for non-flyers in exactly the same way as a wheelchair is a mobility aid for non-walkers.

But that is not the end of it. We spend at least as much money to provide environments, usually called runways and airports, to ensure that these mobility aids can operate without hindrance. Further, hundreds of thousands of people are employed worldwide, in helping non-flyers to overcome their particular mobility difficulties. And finally, in order to provide barrier free environments for non-flyers, we trample on the rights of others, ignoring their pleas not to have their homes bulldozed, their sleep disrupted, or their countryside undisturbed.

Non-walkers are treated in exactly the opposite way. Environments are often designed to exclude us, transport systems that claim to be public continue to deny us access and when we protest, we are told there is no money. We are also told that giving us access to such systems would adversely affect the rights of others; journeys would take longer and would be more expensive for everyone. Perhaps a useful slogan for the next direct action demonstration could be 'equal treatment for non-walkers and non-flyers'.

Of course, it could be argued that not-walking and not-flying are not the same kinds of non-activity; the former affects only a minority, albeit a substantial one, whereas the latter affects everyone. True, but the numbers of non-flyers who are provided with the mobility aids to enable them to fly are even smaller; in other words, in world population terms, flyers are a smaller minority than non-walkers and nearly-walkers. My point is essentially one concerning social justice; treat both groups equally, or at the very least, stop punishing non-walkers and nearly-walkers for not walking.

To conclude then, some of you may have been surprised not simply by what I have said, but also by the way I have attempted to substantiate what I have said. In the world in which we live today, there are few certainties; knowledge, or what counts as knowledge, is both contested and contestable, and objectivity has been rigorously and rightly attacked by the politics of subjectivity.

In both sociology and the study of disability, this is doubly true. So, do not reject my arguments out of hand; if you disagree, contest them. If you think my comments on both elitist and popular culture are unfair, give me non-disablist examples of where disability is handled sensitively. If you think my characterising medical charities as millenarian movements is inappropriate, give me examples of where they have provided cures rather than promises. If you think my description of rehabilitation as control rather than therapy is inaccurate, give me examples of non-controlling rehabilitation.

If Jenny Morris is right when she says 'Disabled people are increasingly challenging the attitude that says that if you cannot walk, then your life isn't worth living' (Morris 1992, p. 3) and I believe that she is, then that challenge faces us all. As Ken Davis put it, we have to put our struggle to create a decent society above our vain attempts to force non-walkers and nearly-walkers to walk. I hope, in addressing the question What's so wonderful about walking? I have made a contribution to this struggle.

# 8
# The World of Disability

## Introduction

This chapter is an attempt to combine two separate but related issues. The first of those is an attempt to, at the very
least, provide an outline sketch of the conditions under which
disabled people live throughout the world. The second, related
issue concerns my puzzlement as to why disabled people, wherever they live, experience conditions of life far worse than their
non-disabled counterparts.

My puzzlement was compounded by the fact that at international and national level, there exist policies, programmes
and legislation which are specifically supposed to address the
poor conditions under which disabled people live throughout
the world. It was not until a few years ago when I was asked to
give a paper at an Economic and Social Research Council spon-
sored seminar on 'Consent and Disabled People' that I began
to put the two issues together. I did this by utilising Gramsci's
notion of consent which I describe more fully later in the
Chapter. Before that it will initially look at the issue of num-

bers and policy responses to disability issues. It will then examine what is known about the material conditions under which disabled people live throughout the world. Finally it will discuss some of the reasons why disabled people remain at the bottom of the pile all over the world and consider the possibilities of improvement.

## The world of disabled people

There are undoubtedly trends to what has been called the 'globalisation' or even the 'macdonaldisation' of society. This is as true in respect of disability as it is other issues facing the world at this time and so a brief review of disability issues in the context of Europeanism and internationalism is, perhaps, appropriate. In undertaking this, it should be borne in mind that the evidence on which it is based is partial as no satisfactory comparative studies have yet been undertaken. Where comparative studies of policy issues in general have been done, disability has remained marginalised and where specific studies of disability policy in different countries have been done, they have become public relations vehicles for individual governments rather than serious academic studies (WHO 1991).

A recent UN report (Despouy 1991) has confirmed earlier estimates that there are more than 500 million impaired persons in the world; that is one in ten of the world's population. The report goes on to suggest that at least '25 per cent of the entire population are adversely affected by the presence of disabilities'. Not everyone would agree with this figure, however, including those international agencies who have responsibility for collecting the appropriate data.

> The ten per cent figure has in any case now been discounted by WHO itself. The author of the WHO Manual on Community-Based Rehabilitation, Dr Hillender, who was responsible for declaring ten per cent to be the world average, now favours about four per cent for developing countries and seven per cent for developed countries.
>
> (Coleridge 1993, p. 108)

Such figures are probably little better than guesswork. There are obviously differences between the developed and developing worlds in both the kinds of impairments produced and the creation of disabilities that result (Oliver 1990). The age structure of populations, the level of technological and medical development, the extent of poverty, the presence or absence of war and the kind of economy are all involved in the production of impairment and the creation of disability. This uncertainty continues to exist despite the investment of large sums of money to produce a classification system to allow for accurate estimates of numbers (Wood 1980). It thus seems clear that the critiques mounted by disabled people over this system have been proved to be correct.

However many disabled people there are, there are clearly enough to come to the attention of the United Nations General Assembly, who adopted the Declaration on the Rights of Disabled Persons in 1975, recommending that all international organisations and agencies should include provisions in their programmes to ensure the effective implementation of these rights and principles. Subsequently 1981 was proclaimed International Year of Disabled Persons with the motto 'Full participation and equality'.

In the following year the UN adopted the World Programme of Action which provided the guidelines for the Decade of Disabled Persons (1983–92) proclaimed by the General Assembly. The aforesaid proclamation makes it clear that 'disabled people have the same rights as others in their societies and that it is the duty of Governments to promote and protect these rights'.

As far as the European Community is concerned, similar uncertainties abound over the numbers of disabled people, although figures for the prevalence of disabled people suggest that approximately ten per cent of the population of the Community were disabled, meaning that there were more than thirty million disabled people residing in Europe.

Policy towards disabled people developed in a more limited way than with the UN. In the 1970s four discrete programme areas developed; an initial action programme to promote the vocational rehabilitation of disabled people; the European Social Fund; a range of supported housing projects; and a programme of activities in the research field. Hopes that such discrete initiatives might form part of a comprehensive social charter of fundamental social rights were dashed in 1989 when such a proposal was watered down to become a 'Community Charter of Basic Social Rights of Workers' (Daunt 1991).

It is difficult to write about the relationship between citizenship and disability in the countries which used to be known as the 'Eastern Block'. What evidence we do have suggests that most of the countries in that block incorporate disability into their constitutions and services are organised primarily to keep people in or return them to the labour force and only after that, are rehabilitation or social care services provided.

However, it needs to be borne in mind that recent upheavals may well mean that old constitutional rights have disappeared along with the 'iron curtain' and the 'Berlin wall'. Equally, as Eastern Europe opens up, evidence is becoming available that despite having constitutional rights, many disabled people experienced profound infringements to their basic human rights.

A recent estimate suggests that in the People's Republic of China, there are 50 million disabled people in a population of 10 billion (Ming 1993). This suggests a prevalence of one in twenty of the population which is about half of the numbers estimated in other parts of the world. This discrepancy could be explained in a number of ways; the difficulties of providing reliable data for such a huge population; different economic and social conditions; higher or lower survival rates amongst disabled people; and so on. The point is that, however reliable the estimates, a substantial number of people in China are disabled.

Little is known about the citizenship rights of disabled people in the People's Republic of China though one visitor summarised the situation thus.

> There is no national social security system or network of personal social services. There are very few mobility aids, and welfare benefits are distributed from the school or workplace. If you are not in school or you are unable to work, then you remain with your family, which does not receive any specific support, or you live in a social welfare institution run by your local Bureau of Civil Affairs.
>
> (Potts 1989, p. 169)

The situation may be beginning to change however. Since Deng Pu Fang, the son of the leader Deng Xiaou Ping, became a paraplegic he is playing an active role in promoting disability issues. In 1990 the Peoples Congress issued a document promoting the rights of disabled people in the area of medical care and rehabilitation, welfare, education and employment.

However, it seems likely that, as in most other parts of the world, Chinese disabled people have yet to see the words translated into reality.

Given these vast numbers of disabled people, we need to consider the material conditions under which disabled people live out their lives and policy responses of governments to these disabled people. Finally, we shall consider why things are as they are and whether they are likely to change.

## The material conditions of disabled people

There have been very few international studies of the lives of disabled people although the UN Report did come to the following conclusion:

> these persons frequently live in deplorable conditions, owing to the presence of physical and social barriers which prevent their integration and full participation in the community. As a result, millions of disabled people throughout the world are segregated and deprived of virtually all their rights, and lead a wretched, marginal life.
>
> (Despouy 1991, p. 1)

It is possible to put some descriptive flesh on the bones of these figures and what follows relies heavily on figures presented in a recent special edition of the *New Internationalist* (No. 233/July 1992) called 'Disabled Lives'.

Of the 500 million disabled people in the world, 300 million live in developing countries, and of these 140 million are children and 160 million are women. One in five, that is one hundred million of the total population of disabled people, are disabled by malnutrition. In the developing countries, only one in a hundred disabled people have access to any form of rehabilitation and 80 per cent of all disabled people live in Asia and the Pacific, but they receive just 2 per cent of the total resources allocated to disabled people. In the third world, the death rate of people with a spinal injury within two years of the injury is as high today as it was in the developed world before the Second World War.

While not being able to put an accurate figure onto it, there is no doubt that, all over the world, there is a close link between disability and poverty.

There is a close relationship between poverty and disability:
malnutrition, mothers weakened by frequent childbirth, inadequate immunisation programmes, accidents in over
crowded homes, all contribute to an incidence of disability
among poor people that is higher than among people living in easier circumstances. Furthermore, disability creates
and exacerbates poverty by increasing isolation and economic
strain, not just for the individual but for the family: there is
little doubt that disabled people are amongst the poorest in
poor countries.

(Coleridge 1993, p. 64)

While in an absolute sense, the material conditions of disabled
people in the developed world is vastly superior to their third
world counterparts, they still experience conditions of life far
inferior to the rest of the population. Thus, for example, more
than 60 per cent of disabled people in both Britain and America
currently live below the poverty line.

Labour markets in the developed world continue to discriminate to the point where disabled people are three times more
likely to be unemployed than their able-bodied counterparts.
In education, the majority of disabled children are still educated in segregated special schools and less than three in a
thousand disabled students end up in higher education, when,
according to prevalence figures, it should be one hundred. On
any indicators, disabled women and black disabled people fare
worse than their white, male counterparts.

While, the accuracy of some of these figures might be called
into question in respect of both the developed and developing world, no one would deny that they paint an authentic
picture of the lives of disabled people throughout the world.
This raises the crucial question. What are governments doing
about it and why?

## Policy responses – citizens of the world?

It would be convenient to be able to apply Marshall's three
aspects of citizenship to this discussion but there are two major
problems with so doing; one conceptual and the other empirical. In conceptual terms, his framework could be accused of
being ethnocentric – that is, dominated by the intellectual tra-
ditions of the West. Thus, for example, political rights cannot

be reduced to enfranchisement. To put it unequivocally, in many parts of the world

> politics is also about civil war, guerilla movements, revolutions, military coups and assassinations, as well as about ballot boxes and speeches in the House of Commons or Senate.
> (Bilton *et al.* 1981, p. 170)

In empirical terms, we simply do not have enough reliable data to make international or European comparisons possible, especially when were are talking about political and social rights. In terms of civil rights, it would be possible to provide in great detail lists of the statutes as they apply to disabled people in each country, but the effects of those statutes on the citizenship of disabled people are difficult to assess.

> The developments in the legal field had a highly positive impact on the social integration of the disabled and on the creation of equal opportunities. Nevertheless, the success of policies aimed at improving the social integration of disabled people is very difficult to judge by any comprehensive or objective measures, even when governments seek to monitor the effect of their policies.
> (Pinet 1990, p. 6)

More specifically, in our discussion of Britain, we need to consider citizenship in the context of rights not to be discriminated against; in other words the pros and cons of anti-discrimination legislation. In recent years many countries have gone down this route, countries as geographically dispersed and politically different as the United States, Sweden and Australia. In Canada, disabled people were included in the Constitution in 1983, and they are specifically included in the recently amended human rights legislation.

It is the recent history of anti-discrimination legislation in the United States which has generated the most attention in this country. Section 504 of the Rehabilitation Act 1973 made it illegal that any disabled person should 'be excluded from participation in, be denied any benefit of, or be subjected to discrimination under any programme or activity receiving federal financial assistance'. It was not merely the fact of the legislation that was significant but also the mass demonstrations and occupation of government buildings by disabled people in Washington DC which were necessary to force a reluctant President to sign the bill.

While the passage of this legislation was a significant event,

> there were many difficulties with the enforcement of the law and doubts about its coverage and effects. The public sector in the United States is much smaller than in many other countries and the fact that the law was restricted to federally funded schemes meant that its effect would be greatly limited, especially when contraction of government spending simply removed the necessary link.
>
> (Bynoe 1991, p. 33)

It therefore became necessary to extend the principle of the Act to other areas and this was done with the passage of the Americans with Disabilities Act in 1990. Again the legislation was only signed after further mass demonstrations of disabled people in Washington, DC. The Act operates in four main areas: employment, public services (including transport), the private sector, and telecommunications.

As the Act has only been fully implemented since 1992, it is too early to make judgements about its efficacy. However opponents argue that unless it's properly resourced its effects may be counter-productive, placing undue financial burdens on organisations and individuals alike. Protagonists argue that the Act will pay for itself in that by reducing employment discrimination, it will both raise tax revenues and reduce welfare payments. Further, opening up access to goods and services to disabled people will stimulate new demand in the economy.

The relationship between education and citizenship is also important, as I have already argued, while the relationship between educational inclusion and other entitlements of citizenship is not a simple one, and the problems of making cross-national comparisons persist. Daunt (1991), who was the first head of the European Commission's Bureau for Action in Favour of Disabled People, divides the member states into the following four categories: first, radical integration in countries like Italy and Denmark; second, the gradualist approach in countries like France and the United Kingdom; third, the conservative tradition within Germany and the Netherlands; and fourth, the countries like Spain who are, only now, developing their special education system and others who have not yet begun the process.

While such a classification is a crude comparison, it is intended to be descriptive and it cannot be inferred that radical integration equals citizenship. Further, each of these member states will have different legislative approaches to other areas such as health, welfare, social security and the like, and it is therefore impossible to infer any simplistic relationship between the degree of inclusion in education and the degree of inclusion in the rest of life.

Fulcher (1989), in comparing educational systems in Britain, the United States, Denmark and Australia, suggests that all four operate a discourse of integration and rights. However, she concludes that the only country which successfully translates this discourse into policy and practice is Denmark. The other three fail because they focus on change at the policy level, whereas Denmark has been much more concerned to develop an integrative pedagogy. From this it cannot be concluded that if the other three countries switched from policy to pedagogy, that integration would be achieved; that would not necessarily be the case for the reasons suggested above; namely that inclusion in education, however achieved, cannot be seen in isolation.

In considering these cross-national issues, the question of which country offers disabled people the best chance of citizenship is often legitimately asked. From the evidence presented here, there is no simple answer to such a question – no country has got it completely right and all initiatives need to take into account the differing economic, social, political and cultural context.

Even in Europe as the Action Programme for Disabled People went into a second phase in 1988, the first official report on its progress recognised that 'disabled people form one of the most disadvantaged groups in the population' (Daunt 1991, p. 151). And the former Head of the Action Bureau for Disabled Persons forcefully argues that legal protection to redress this problem is necessary throughout the Community:

> The idea that disadvantaged groups in our society will ever get a fair deal until their equal rights are legally guaranteed, for the whole range of services and sectors within which the disadvantage operates, is so contrary to common sense

and to the universal experience of human conduct that it can only be tendentious.

(Daunt 1991, p. 185)

While this may be true for the developed world, the value of such legislative programmes both to the developing world and to that part of the world we used to call Eastern Europe, will need to be critically examined as will attempts to export Western social care provision and rehabilitation programmes. According to one commentator, Western advisers, while they abound in goodwill and rhetoric understand little of the realities of rehabilitation planning in the Third World. Not only that, but

> Asian counterparts of Western advisers have mostly been too polite ... or they have themselves had no better idea than the sort of top down, fragmented, profession dominated, gadget-bound scheme that has too often been foisted onto the third world by proselytisers for various dubious methodologies.
>
> (Miles 1989, p. 117)

And he ends with the sanguine reminder that for 'most disabled people, the International Decade will pass without trace'.

## Why – the organisation of consent?

In addressing the question of why, we need to turn to the work of Gramsci (1971). He suggested that the survival of capitalism depends upon the consent of the overwhelming majority of people, whose real interests lie in its overthrow. This consent, he went on to suggest, was both organised by one group and acquiesced to by another. Whether the real interests of disabled people lie in the overthrow of capitalism is beyond the scope of this chapter, but in a more limited sense, Gramsci's notion of consent does help to explain the situation referred to earlier; namely the continued appalling material conditions under which the vast majority of disabled people live despite major policies and programmes supposedly designed to alleviate these material conditions and ensure the rights of citizenship.

Consent is organised in a number of ways. To begin with, it is organised through the ideology of personal tragedy theory. This promotes the idea that disability can happen to anyone;

that it occurs as a chance event, and that anyone, anywhere at any time, can become disabled. Of course, when one looks at the evidence, it is clear that this view is merely ideological. Like other social and economic inequalities, the acquisition of an individual impairment is related to a whole range of material factors like geography, age, class, gender and race. To put the matter succinctly, you are far more likely to be disabled if you are a young or old black working-class woman living in the third world than a white middle-class man living in Britain or the United States.

A second way in which consent is organised is through the promotion of supposed humanitarian social policies and programmes. Earlier, I mentioned some of these at the international level; the UN Declaration of the Rights of Disabled Persons and the World Programme of Action to name but two. Similar situations abound at the national level with the production of reports and charters.

There is an added dimension to this as well; the promotion of these policies and programmes through legislation. Britain has a record in this area with the National Assistance Act (1948), the Chronically Sick and Disabled Persons Act (1970), the Disabled Persons (Services, Consultation and Representation) Act (1986), the National Health Service and Community Care Act (1990) as well as additional clauses attached to general social policy legislation. Again, there is little evidence to show that this legislation has substantially improved the material conditions under which disabled people continue to live.

In terms used here, this could be called the State organisation of consent at international and national level. The State further organises this consent in a less direct way through the establishment and ongoing support of a whole range of intermediary organisations. Rehabilitation International and the Action Bureau for the Disabled are examples at the international level, and they often spawn their own programmes variously called HELIOS, TIDE, Handynet and so on.

A plethora of similar organisations exist at the national level; in Britain such organisations are often given Royal approval and those who don't have it often spend more time attempting to obtain it than meeting the needs of their members. The point is that the existence of such organisations is part of the organisation of consent. They perpetuate the myth that society cares about disabled people because these organisations exist to promote our interests. The reality is that the only interests they promote are the State's and their own.

A third way in which consent is organised is through medical and therapeutic intervention in our lives. This intervention begins before birth through attempts to screen out certain 'conditions' or to develop genetic engineering, and continues throughout the life of disabled people in their encounters with the therapeutic state and the professionals who operate it. Cohen makes the general point that

> professionals and experts continue to increase their monopolistic reach and their ability to make people dependent upon them – in health, education, welfare, life-styles, family policy, deviancy control.
>
> (Cohen 1985, p. 164)

There are two dangers with this. Firstly, as Morris (1992) has pointed out, disabled people are being excluded by the medical and scientific community from the debate about which society is healthier; the one which seeks to eradicate disease, illness and pathology or the one which seeks to welcome and celebrate difference. Secondly, there are no limits to the therapeutic state (Kittrie 1971) and the kind of society it may produce.

> A profession and a society which are so concerned with physical and functional wellbeing as to sacrifice civil liberty and moral integrity must inevitably press for a scientific environment similar to that provided for laying hens on progressive chicken farms – hens who produce eggs industriously and have no disease or other cares.
>
> (Freidson 1970, p. 356)

While, as one commentator has pointed out

> Disabled people are in the process of liberating themselves from another force which has constrained them for centuries: the medical profession. Doctors and paramedics colonized disability, and turned disabled people into material for research and experimentation.
>
> (Baird 1992, p. 5)

It remains true, that medical and therapeutic intervention is a key force in the organisation of consent.

Returning to Gramsci's conception of consent, he suggested it was not something that was only organised from above; it required the acquiesence of those below. So why do disabled people consent? In the first place, the material conditions under which disabled people live throughout the world make disability an isolating experience. If you're poor, if you don't have enough to eat, if you're kept in seclusion by State or family, if little of society's public spaces or wealth are accessible to you, then it is small wonder that disabled people find it difficult to organise collectively in order to withdraw their consent.

But it goes further than that. Precisely because disability in all parts of the world is an isolating experience, most disabled people only experience their disabilities in individual terms. Thus, they may internalise the ideology of personal tragedy, they may come to see themselves as a burden and feel that their problems are their own fault. And in terms of the propaganda that some charities put out (Hevey 1992), it is no surprise that disabled people may come to take on this view.

There is a further reason that disabled people consent. The policies and programmes that are promoted as being in our interests are, in reality, nothing of the kind. As Wolfensberger (1989) has pointed out, 'human services' in what he calls 'post primary production economies' are deliberately designed to create dependency. This he suggests is because the real purpose of the services is to give employment to the ever growing middle classes rather than to meet the needs of disadvantaged or deprived people. While there is some element of truth in this, I would suggest that the 'really' real purpose that these services serve, is that they are a key element in the organisation of consent.

Finally, this really real purpose is often given a spurious reality by the fact that disabled people appear to 'consent' to these services. If we take day centres as an example; it is certainly true that many disabled people choose to go to them but is that choice really real? When the alternative, because of discriminatory labour markets and inaccessible public spaces, is to stay at home in isolation, increase your heating bills and watch daytime soaps on television, small wonder many disabled people appear to consent. But how many disabled people would continue to consent if they were given the money it costs to keep the day centres open?

## Will disabled people continue to consent?

All over the world, disabled people are increasingly coming to realise that our own emancipation is in our hands. We cannot rely on others, whoever they are and whatever their motives, for that is the road to the gas chamber, the residential institution, the hospital and extermination before birth. Creating our own organisations is not something to take our minds off our 'tragedies' but a matter of life or death. Our numerical strength described below has to be translated into action, even if that action means withdrawing our consent from what is happening to us.

> In 10 years, membership of BCODP has risen to include over 80 member groups, whilst DPI is currently made up of over 70 national assemblies, all run by disabled people. Membership of both is still growing.
>
> (Davis 1993, p. 285)

In terms of policies and programmes, this growing disability movement has turned away from the professionally dominated top down solutions provided by able-bodied experts; programmes dependent upon expensive professional labour, new technology, hardware, software and the like. Instead it has advocated policies based upon according disabled people full citizenship rights through anti-discrimination legislation and programmes designed to facilitate independence through the promotion of personal assistance schemes.

Further, the movement has sought to develop links with other issues; DPI, for example, has always seen the Peace Movement as close to its heart, simply because war regularly creates millions of people with impairments.

> New groups have emerged to address new issues; GEMMA raised the concerns of disabled lesbians. The Liberation Network of People with Disabilities focused on the issue of social attitudes, personal growth and awareness raising. Sisters Against Disablement began to address the double oppression of disabled women, and Disabled People Against Apartheid was set up in solidarity with black people in South Africa.
>
> (Davis 1993, pp. 288–9)

In addition, the movement has begun to challenge the ideology of personal tragedy theory through the development of 'disability arts'. This has produced writing, poetry, songs, theatre, art as well as its own organisations and journals. Its aim is to celebrate difference and produce its own disability culture.

Finally, as well as using the usual political tactics for raising issues, the disability movement has used other tactics such as mass demonstrations and direct action over issues such as stopping the war in Lebanon, inaccessible public transport, negative media imagery and pedestrianisation. Organisation to facilitate such developments have also come into being including ADAPT in the USA, and CAT, CSP and DAN in Britain. While such tactics may appear new, Hasler points out that 'A mixture of direct action and parliamentary lobbying is not new: the National League of the Blind used this method in 1933' (Hasler 1993, p. 283). This story of the growth and diversification of the international disability movement over the past few years is even more remarkable when it is realised that all this has been achieved despite chronic underfunding by national states, and by the international community. To return to the terms that Gramsci might have used, states and governments have clearly demonstrated that they prefer to fund the organisation of consent rather than the organisation of discontent.

## Conclusion

As we approach the end of the twentieth century it is possible to see both positive and negative forces shaping the world-wide destiny of disabled people into the twenty-first century, both of which have been discussed in this chapter. The positive forces centre upon our abilities to continue to organise our movement at local, national and international level. The negative forces are the continued oppression and exploitation that continues unchecked all over the world.

As far as disabled people are concerned, our very lives are threatened not just by physical attacks from neo-fascist movements but also from policies developed by our governments. Compulsory abortions in China, euthanasia in Holland, and quality of life debates all over the world pose threats to our very existence. Lest we in Britain think that all this is happening elsewhere, we should remember that:

The Nazi doctors declared at the Nuremburg Trials that they were doing no more than doctors everywhere did, but without official sanction. Nowadays, when market forces are the dominant factor shaping social policies, it is not uncommon for doctors and health planners to argue that 'the country cannot afford too many disabled people'. The medical profession and planners of health services are ambivalent about the wonders of modern medicine: it can prolong the life of, for example, a person with spina bifida, but at what cost to the exchequer? And what if they have children? Who will pay for the consequences?.

(Coleridge 1993, p. 46)

# 9

# Understanding the Hegemony of Disability

## Introduction

The original version of this chapter was written in response to an invitation to Gerry Zarb and myself to present some findings of research we had recently completed on ageing with a spinal injury at an international conference in Denver, Colorado. Initially we were to do a joint presentation but subsequently we were asked to present separate papers which took into account theoretical developments and policy contexts.

I don't remember why I ended up writing the theoretical one except that it gave me the opportunity to review work I had undertaken over the past fifteen years. In looking at this, I found that my work could be divided into three areas; attempts to develop social theory; attempts to make sense of experience by linking them to concepts derived from what one sociologist (Merton 1968) has called 'middle range theorising'; and attempts to develop emancipatory forms of academic practice. The invitation enabled me to consider what had so far been done but also clearly showed that I had not got very far in linking the three areas together. This chapter then, is the most recent, but by no means last, attempt to explore these links.

## Disability production in transition

Whatever the fate of disabled people before the advent of capitalist society and whatever their fate will be in the brave new world of the twenty-first century, with its coming they suffered economic and social exclusion. As a consequence of this exclusion disability was produced in a particular form; as an individual problem requiring medical treatment. Old age suffered a similar fate.

The transition to late capitalism (the post-industrial society as some writers have called it or its more recent fashionable manifestation as post-modernity) has led to demands for the inclusion of those previously excluded. As a consequence of this, the production of disability as an individual medical problem has increasingly come under attack and attempts to produce disability in a different, social form commensurate with inclusion, has been appearing upon the societal agenda.

Before proceeding further, it is perhaps necessary to explain the use of terminology in this chapter. Underpinning it is a materialist view of society; to say that the category disability (or ageing or any other social category) is produced by capitalist society in a particular form implies a particular world view. Within this world view, the production of the category disability is no different from the production of motor cars or hamburgers. Each has an industry, whether it be the car, fast food or human service. Each industry has a workforce which has a vested interest in producing its own product in particular ways and in exerting as much control over the process of production as possible.

The production of disability in one sense, therefore, is nothing more nor less than a set of activities specifically geared towards producing a good – the category disability – supported by a range of political actions which create the conditions to allow these productive activities to take place and underpinned by a discourse which gives legitimacy to the whole enterprise. This chapter is part of an attempt to produce the category disability in a new form; an attempt which stems from disabled people themselves.

In order to understand societal responses to long-term disability, it is necessary to understand that the production of disability is in transition. In this process of transition, the move away from an individualised, medical view of disability does not imply that there is no role for medicine in the world to which we are moving. Clearly part of the experience of disability will remain an individual one. But in order to develop more appropriate societal responses to disability, it is important that we all understand – politicians, policy makers, professionals, the public and disabled people alike – that this is a partial and limited view. Our complex and difficult task is to understand that this process is one of transition from one world view of disability to another. This process is what Kuhn (1961) would call a 'paradigm shift'.

There are three basic levels at which we can approach this task; the ontological, the epistemological and the experiential. In other words: what is the nature of the disability? what causes it? and how is it experienced? These basic questions raise different sets of issues at different levels of abstraction. The ontological level requires issues to be addressed in terms of grand theory, examples of which would include the work of Parsons (1951) and Marx (1913). The epistemological level requires issues to be addressed in terms of middle range theorising, the need for which was pointed to in the work of American sociologist Merton (1968). The experiential level requires issues to be addressed in terms of developing an appropriate methodology for understanding the experience of disability from the perspective of disabled people themselves (Campling 1981; Oliver *et al.* 1988; Morris 1989).

These levels do not exist independently of each other except in a conceptual sense. Rather, they interact with each other in producing what might be called the totality, or indeed, the

TABLE 9.1 The hegemony of disability

| Level | Question | Way of understanding |
|---|---|---|
| Ontology | What is the nature of disability? | Grand theory |
| Epistemology | What causes disability? | Middle range theories? |
| Experience | What does it feel like to be disabled? | Methodology |

hegemony of disability. Hegemony, as it is used here describes the ways in which the ontological level, the epistemological and the experiential levels interconnect with each other to form a complete whole. Like the concept of consent, it is borrowed from the work of Antonio Gramsci (Bocock 1987).

The hegemony of disability, as it is produced by capitalist society – and it should be emphasised that other kinds of society have produced disability in different forms (for examples of the production of disability in different cultural forms, see Oliver 1990, esp. Chapter 2) – stems from the ontological assumptions it makes about the pathological and problem-oriented nature of disability.

These ontological assumptions link directly to epistemological concerns about the causes of disability in individuals with a view to eradication through prevention, cure or treatment. Hence the assumption is, in health terms, that disability is pathology and in welfare terms, that disability is a social problem. Treatment and cure are the appropriate societal responses to pathologies and problems. Finally these assumptions and concerns exert a considerable influence on the way disability is experienced by both able-bodied and disabled people alike – to have a disability is to have a problem, to have a disability is to have 'something wrong with you'.

In recent years, the hegemony of disability has been under a sustained and persistent attack in late capitalist society. At the ontological level this has led, not to a denial of the problem-oriented nature of disability, but of its assumptions of pathology. At the epistemological level middle range theorising has been turned on its head; disability is caused not by the functional, physical or psychological limitations of impaired individuals but by the failure of society to remove its disabling barriers and social restrictions. At the experiential level disabled people are increasingly seeing their problems as stemming from social oppression (Sutherland 1981) and institutionalised discrimination (Barnes 1991). In other words, disability is something wrong with society.

Thus the argument that the problems of disability are societal rather than individual problems and that these problems stem from oppression by society rather than the limitations of individuals is an essential part of developing an understanding of societal responses to long-term disability. Further, there is plenty of evidence to show that most policy and practice in this area has failed because it has been based upon individual rather than social models of disability (Oliver 1983; Borsay 1986); the individual model being a product of exclusion, the social model currently being produced by demands for inclusion.

However, in attempting to understand hegemony of disability, the ways in which the individualising of disability is interconnected at the levels of society, policy and practice, and personal experience is crucial. These interconnections are crucial to the attempt to reformulate disability as an issue for society and develop a more appropriate social understanding of policy responses, professional practice and personal experience.

The individualising of disability permeates all three levels and connects them in that disability is seen as a personal tragedy which occurs at random to individuals, that the problems of disability require individuals to adjust or come to terms with this tragedy and that research has used techniques designed to 'prove' the existence of these adjustment problems. The alternative view suggests that disability occurs in structured ways dependent upon the material relations of production (Oliver 1990), the problem of adjustment is one for society, not individuals and that research should be concerned with identifying the ways in which society disables people rather than the effects on individuals (Oliver 1992, a; Zarb 1992).

Critiques of both the dominant way of understanding disability and the alternative formulation will be discussed in what follows and can be summarised in Table 9.2.

TABLE 9.2　Exclusionary and inclusionary visions

| Way of understanding | Dominant | Alternative |
|---|---|---|
| Grand theory | Personal tragedy | Political economy |
| Middle range theories | Adjustment/ Disengagement | Social adjustment |
| Methodology | Positivist/ Interpretive | Emancipatory |

## Grand theory – personal tragedy or political economy?

Grand theory, in sociological terms, is concerned with providing an all-embracing explanation of particular phenomena at the highest level of abstraction. Undoubtedly, in terms of the phenomenon of disability, the dominant grand theory has been personal tragedy theory. This suggests that disability is a tragic happening that occurs to unfortunate, isolated individuals on a random basis. It further influences compensatory policy responses and therapeutic interventions designed to help individuals come to terms with tragedy. At the level of individual experience, many disabled people come to see their lives as blighted by tragedy.

The problem is that personal tragedy theory does not provide a universalistic explanation of disability; in some societies disability is seen as the ascription of privilege, as a sign of being chosen by the gods (Hanks and Hanks 1980). In others it is seen as bringing important social benefits such as bilingualism, as illustrated by the pervasive use of sign language throughout the community that was Martha's Vineyard (Groce 1985). Further, even within some capitalist societies policies are moving away from compensation and towards entitlement. Therapeutic interventions are also moving away from adjustment and towards empowerment. Finally, with the developing of a politics of personal identity, the experience of disability is being reinterpreted in positive rather than negative terms (Morris 1991).

Political economy, on the other hand, suggests that all phenomena (including social categories) are produced by the economic and social forces of capitalism itself. The forms in which they are produced are ultimately dependent upon their relationship to the economy (Marx 1913).

Hence, both the categories of ageing and disability are produced in the particular forms they appear by these very economic and social forces. Further, they are produced as an economic problem because of changes in the nature of work and the needs of the labour market within capitalism, and this is true of both ageing and disability separately.

> The political economy perspective points to the structural dependency of the aged arising from conditions in the labour market and the stratification and organisation of work and society.
>
> (Estes 1984, p. 30)

In other words, old people no longer play a key role in the process of production and no longer participate in the labour market.

The same is true of disabled people and has been so, except in times of severe labour shortage, since the coming of
the industrial revolution.

> The speed of factory work, the enforced discipline, the time-
> keeping and production norms – all these were a highly
> unfavourable change from the slower, more self-determined
> methods of work into which many handicapped people had
> been integrated.
>
>                                   (Ryan and Thomas 1980, p. 101)

Hence the economy, through both the operation of the labour
market and the social organisation of work, plays a key role in
determining societal responses not just to ageing and disability but also to ageing with a disability. Both old people and
disabled people are forced into situations of dependency (Oliver
1989b; Walker 1980) because they do not participate fully in
the processes of production. However, it would be wrong to
assume that old disabled people simply experience a double
dose of dependency; to put the matter simply, to be old and
disabled is not twice as bad as merely being old or merely disabled (this issue, conceptualised as 'simultaneous oppression',
is discussed further later in the chapter).

In order to explain this, it is necessary to return to the crucial question of what is meant by political economy and whether
it is possible to have separate political economies of ageing
and disability, or indeed race, gender, welfare or any other
category. The following is a generally agreed definition of political economy,

> The study of the interrelationships between the polity,
> economy and society, or more specifically, the reciprocal in-
> fluences among government . . . the economy, social classes,
> state and, status groups. The central problem of the politi-
> cal economy perspective is the manner in which the economy
> and polity interact in a relationship of reciprocal causation
> affecting the distribution of social goods.
>
>                                         (Estes *et al.* 1982)

There are two problems with such an agreed definition. To
begin with, it is an explanation which can be incorporated into
pluralist visions of society as a consensus emerging out of the

interests of various groups and social forces and indeed, this explanation has been encapsulated in a recent book on disability (Albrecht 1992). In addition, such political economies often themselves become oppressive in that they divide up the experiences into an arbitrary set of socially constructed categories; old age, race, gender, disability, etc.

Political economy, as it is used here, takes a particular theoretical view of society; one which sees the economy as the crucial, and ultimately determining factor, in structuring the lives of groups and individuals. Further, while the relationship between various groups and the economy may differ in qualitative ways, the underlying structural relationship remains.

> ... racism, sexism, ageism and economic imperialism are all oppressive 'isms' and built-in responses of a society that considers certain groups inferior. All are rooted in the social-economic structures of society. All deprive certain groups of status, the right to control their own lives and destinies with the end result of powerlessness. All have resulted in economic and social discrimination. All rob [American] society of the energies and involvement of creative persons who are needed to make our society just and humane. All have brought on individual alienation, despair, hostility, and anomie.
>
> (Walton 1979, p. 9)

As is usual in discussing the oppressions for which isms become shorthand, disablism does not merit inclusion. The reason for this is simple; even those writers who have specifically examined oppression have internalised the dominant, individualised world view of disability and have failed to conceptualise it as social oppression. Equally importantly, such theorising about oppression leaves the relationship between the various isms as non-problematic; with the exception of Abberley (1987) there have been no attempts to analyse the similarities and differences between the oppressions of disability, race and gender.

The 'politics' part of political economy comes in the ways in which ageing and disability are constructed as particular kinds of problems. Any society wishing to appear 'civilised' must make provision for those groups and individuals who cannot provide for their own needs through work (Stone 1985) or resources built up through previous work (Oliver 1991, a). Hence both ageing and disability are socially constructed as 'problems'.

Earlier it was suggested that producers of categories have an interest in shaping the ways they are produced. Both disability and old age are constructed as social problems because of the needs of the welfare system and the professionals who operate it rather than the needs of old disabled people (Phillipson 1982; Zarb and Oliver 1993). Both are constructed as health problems because of the needs of the health care system and because of the imperialism of the medical profession which has proclaimed a whole range of social phenomena from crime to homosexuality through addiction and onto naughtiness in children as problems requiring medical intervention (Illich 1975; Conrad and Schneider 1980).

## Middle range theory – adjustment, disengagement or social adjustment?

Middle range theories are usually concerned to link the abstract concepts of grand theory to the specific experiences of particular phenomena. In terms of ageing and disability, loss has been the dominant metaphor for developing these perspectives. They have been operationalised in the study of ageing in terms of middle range disengagement theories and in the study of disability in terms of middle range adjustment theories. A critique of each will be provided before attempting to summarise recent work on social adjustment.

Until recently, the field of gerontology – the systematic study of ageing – has been dominated by theories which sought to explain how individuals react to the ageing process. Firstly, there are a range of individualist and psychological models which are primarily preoccupied with explaining 'normal' and/or 'successful' ageing – i.e. adaptation to old age. Here, ageing is viewed as part of an ordered life process moving from birth to death, with each stage (e.g. adolescence, early adulthood, etc.) having its own set of expectations and behaviours (Neugarten and Hagestad 1976). From this perspective, successful adaptation to ageing is represented by an individual accepting the changes that he or she has experienced and, ultimately, accepting the inevitability of death. At the same time, failure to undergo such change is often taken as evidence of pathological personality development (Reichard 1968).

One of the most influential models of ageing has been disengagement theory. This theory suggests that the life course is marked by stages such as 'young old age', 'middle old age' and 'old old age'. Here, the main emphasis is on 'social roles' rather than personal psychology. From this perspective, ageing is characterised by various patterns of 'disengagement' whereby

> as people grow older their behaviour changes, the activities that characterize them in middle age become curtailed, and the extent of their social interaction decreases.
>
> (Havighurst *et al.* 1968, p. 61)

These developmental approaches to ageing have a certain usefulness in that they focus on individual experiences over the totality of the life course. There are several reasons, however, why theories based on disengagement and role change do not provide an adequate analytic framework for studying the experiences of ageing with disability.

Firstly, the models of ageing implicit in these theories take little or no account of social factors which are external to individual psychological states or interpersonal behaviour such as the levels of pensions paid or the social attitudes to ageing. Secondly, ageing is usually conceptualised in terms of an inevitable and pathological process; consequently, older people are viewed as victims lacking control over their own lives. These theories do not, therefore, take account of individual differences in attitudes, expectations and resources. All of these factors may have a significant effect on how any one individual may experience ageing – either positively or negatively (Brearley 1982).

Apart from these conceptual objections to such theories, it is important to note that much of the existing research evidence indicates that the experiences of many older people simply do not match the kind of experience predicted. A major research study of ageing in three countries (Shanas *et al.* 1968) showed that the majority of older people – given good health and adequate financial resources – do not experience a significant reduction in the scope of their activities, as disengagement theory would predict. More recent studies have also indicated that, where it does occur, any reduction in social involvement is much more closely associated with infirmity and poverty, than with age itself (Harris 1983). In other words, if some older people are less socially active, it is due to these external social factors which vary independently of chronological age. Because the individualistic approaches to ageing do not take sufficient account of factors external to the individual, they make the basic error of assuming the observable association between such problems and old age are actually caused by ageing itself.

Just as studies on ageing have been dominated by middle range disengagement theories, so studies of disability have been dominated by middle range adjustment theories. The argument suggests that when something happens to an individual's body something happens to the mind as well. Thus, in order to become fully human again, in order to form a disabled identity, the disabled individual must undergo medical treatment and physical rehabilitation as well as the process of psychological adjustment or coming to terms with disability (Finkelstein 1980).

However, the conceptual framework provided by middle range adjustment theory has been severely criticised on theoretical grounds (Oliver 1981) as well as on the grounds that it does not accord with the actual experience of disability and alternative frameworks such as social adjustment (Oliver *et al.* 1988) and social oppression (UPIAS 1976) have been developed. But it is not just disabled people who have provided theoretical and experiential criticisms of this framework, researchers also have found it difficult to provide empirical evidence:

> Our view of the available literature suggests that a great deal of variability exists in individual reactions to negative life events, both within a particular life crisis and across different crises. We have found little reliable evidence to indicate that people go through stages of emotional responses following an undesirable life event. We have also reviewed a substantial body of evidence suggesting that a large minority of victims of aversive life events experience distress or disorganisation long after recovery might be expected. Current theoretical models of reactions to aversive outcomes cannot account for the variety of responses that appear.
>
> (Silver and Wortman 1980, p. 309)

Initial work on the long-term effects of spinal cord injury suggested that the occurrence of a disability as a significant event in an individual's life is only a starting point for understanding the practical and personal consequences of living with disability. The work further suggested that the social environment, material resources and – most importantly – the meanings which individuals attach to situations and events were the most important factors to be considered in developing an adequate conceptual model which has been called social adjustment.

> For us, then, understanding the consequences of spinal cord injury involves a complex relationship between the impaired individual, the social context within which the impairment occurs and the meanings available to individuals to enable them to make sense of what is happening.
>
> (Oliver *et al.* 1988, p. 11)

In a subsequent study on ageing, this basic approach has been built on to consider the longer term experiences of people who are ageing with a spinal cord injury. As previously, the concepts of 'significant life events' and 'career' are essential components in the conceptual model being developed. Before proceeding, therefore, it is necessary to explain what is meant by these terms and how they have been used in previous work.

While much of the existing work which has utilised the concept of life events has focused on negative life events (Mechanic 1962), there is no logical reason why it cannot be applied to positive aspects of people's life experience. The only essential criteria are that a life event should be disrupting or have the potential to disrupt (Dohrenwend and Dohrenwend 1974) and, that this should have some significant meaning for the individual (Brown and Harris 1979). This means that a whole range of life events can be considered including leaving school, working, marriage, having children, getting divorced, losing one's job as well, of course, as the range of life events often associated with ageing (e.g. retirement, the death of a spouse, etc.).

Since the understanding of the significance of ageing for older disabled people has been a central concern, the concept of life events provides a very useful conceptual tool. However, it is not a matter of simply being concerned with understanding the significance of life events associated with ageing in isolation from people's previous experiences and future expectations. Thus, just as the occurrence of a spinal cord injury is not simply a single, isolated event, so the intervening impact of ageing cannot be considered as a self-contained life event, or even as a series of discrete life events.

Consequently, the concept of career is a further essential component of the model as it allows consideration of people's experiences throughout their lives including, but not restricted to, their experiences of disability and, subsequently, ageing with a disability. Equally importantly, and this relates back to a point made in the previous section, using the concept of career does not require the experiences of ageing and those of disability to be conceptually or experientially discrete and separate.

The concept of 'career' as an aid to the analysis of life experiences was developed by the American sociologists Strauss and Glaser (1967, 1975) and has subsequently been used in a variety of contexts such as education, work experience and marriage, as well as in some studies of the experiences of disabled people (Safilios-Rothschild 1970; Blaxter 1980). The main utility of the concept of a 'disability career' is that it focuses not only on the experience of disability, but also on the interaction between this and other aspects of an individual's total life experience (Carver 1982).

The concept of social adjustment was developed both to link together the concepts of life events and career and to facilitate an understanding of the wide variety of personal responses to spinal injury:

> understanding the consequences of SCI involves a complex relationship between the impaired individual, the social context within which the impairment occurs and the meanings available to individuals to enable them to make sense of what is happening. This is what we mean by social adjustment; it is more than simply the functional limitations that an individual has or the social restrictions encountered; it is a complex relationship between impairment, social restrictions and meaning.
>
> (Oliver *et al.* 1988, p. 11)

The experience of spinal cord injury, therefore, cannot be understood in terms of purely internal psychological or inter-personal processes, but requires a whole range of other material factors such as housing, finance, employment, the built environment and family circumstances to be taken into account. Further all of these material factors can and will change over time, sometimes for the better and sometimes for the worse, hence giving the experience of disability a temporal as well as a material dimension.

Hence the personal responses of individuals to their disabilities cannot be understood merely as a reaction to trauma or tragedy but have to be located in a framework which takes account of their life histories, their material circumstances and the meaning their disability has for them; in sum, social adjustment.

## Methodology – interpreting or understanding the experience of disability?

The central methodological issue concerns the purpose of research and whether this is to interpret or understand particular phenomena. As far as disability research is concerned, most has gone for the interpretive approach but the problem is that it has been located within the medical model with its in-built positivistic assumptions which see disability as individual pathology, rather than the social model of disability, as articulated by disabled people themselves, which sees disability as social restriction or oppression. Consequently, most of this research is considered at best irrelevant, and at worst, oppressive (Oliver 1987).

The persistent lack of fit between able-bodied and disabled people's own articulations of their own experience has implications for both the provision of services and the ability of individuals to control their own lives. As Davis (1986) points out, research on disability has consistently failed to involve disabled people except as passive objects for interviews and observations designed by researchers with no experience or sensitivity to the day-to-day reality of disability – a situation which, whilst it may be of benefit to researchers, does nothing to serve the interests of disabled people. Thus many disabled people have become alienated from disability research; a not uncommon problem for research subjects, according to one commentator (Rowan 1981).

The term alienation in its original Marxist sense referred to the process of labour whereby workers became estranged from the products they produced. In a powerful critique of most of what passes for social research, Rowan argues that alienation is the outcome of the process of this research. By this he meant

treating people as fragments. This is usually done by putting a person into the role of 'research subject' and only then permitting a very restricted range of behaviour to be counted.

This is alienating because it is using the person for someone else's ends – the person's actions do not belong to that
individual, but to the researcher and the research plan.

(Rowan 1981, p. 93)

Hence, attempting to separate out people's experience of ageing with a disability in order to provide services organised on
the basis of the assumption that the two are separable, is, itself
alienating.

The recent history of disability research, in Great Britain at
least, can certainly be seen in the terms described above. The
national disability survey undertaken by the Office of Population Censuses and Surveys (OPCS) on behalf of the British
Government is a good example of such alienation. Since the
publication of the findings of this research (Martin, Meltzer
and Elliot 1988; Martin and White 1988), despite promises to
the contrary, the Government has failed to take any coherent
policy initiatives based upon it. OPCS has not taken it further,
considering that they have done what they were contracted to
do. Disabled people and their organisations have either ignored
it or disputed both its reliability and validity (DIG 1988; Disability Alliance 1988; Abberley 1991).

Much of this was predictable in advance because of the alienation of disabled people from the process of research. They
were not consulted about the research in advance; what issues
should be investigated, how the research should be carried out
and so on. Further, in Rowan's terms, the researchers and the
researched were alienated from each other in the way the research was carried out. Disabled people either filled in a postal
questionnaire or were interviewed, not by the principal OPCS
workers but by part-time interviewers. Further,

It is in the nature of the interview process that the inter-
viewer presents as expert and the disabled person as an
isolated individual inexperienced in research, and thus
unable to reformulate the questions in a more appropriate
way. It is hardly surprising that, by the end of the interview,
the disabled person has come to believe that his or her
problems are caused by their own health/disability problems
rather than by the organisation of society. It is in this sense
that the process of the interview is oppressive, reinforcing
onto isolated, individual disabled people the idea that the

problems they experience in everyday living are a direct result of their own personal inadequacies or functional limitations.

(Oliver 1992a, p. 105)

Hence the research experience for all concerned was an isolating, individual one reinforcing the dominant idea of disability as an individual problem. Finally, according to Abberley (1991) it attempted to 'depoliticise the unavoidably political, to examine the complex and subtle through crude and simplistic measures'.

This alienation from the most extensive and most expensive disability research ever carried out in Britain is not simply an isolated example but symptomatic of a wider crisis that exists between disabled people and the research community. As disabled people have increasingly analysed their segregation, inequality and poverty in terms of discrimination and oppression, research has been seen as part of the problem rather than as part of the solution. Disabled people have come to see research as a violation of their experience, as irrelevant to their needs and as failing to improve their material circumstances and quality of life.

This disillusion with existing research paradigms has raised the issue of developing an alternative, emancipatory approach in order to make disability research both more relevant to the lives of disabled people and more influential in improving their material circumstances. The two key fundamentals on which such an approach must be based are empowerment and reciprocity. These fundamentals can be built in by encouraging self-reflection and a deeper understanding of the research situation by the research subjects themselves as well as enabling researchers to identify with their research subjects (Lather 1987, 1991).

The importance of emancipatory research, therefore,

is in establishing a dialogue between research workers and the grass-roots people with whom they work, in order to discover and realise the practical and cultural needs of those people. Research here becomes one part of a developmental process including also education and political action.

(Reason 1988, p. 2)

Such an understanding is an essential pre-requisite to providing a re-definition of 'the real nature of the problem'. This process has been succinctly captured in a commentary on research on black issues.

> It was not black people who should be examined, but white society; it was not a case of educating blacks and whites for integration, but of fighting institutional racism; it was not race relations that was the field for study, but racism.
>
> (Bourne 1980, p. 339)

This quote, ten years later, applies exactly to the 'state' of disability research: it is not disabled people who need to be examined but able-bodied society; it is not a case of educating disabled and able-bodied people for integration, but of fighting institutional disablism; it is not disability relations which should be the field for study but disablism.

But since we cannot study disablism, or racism or sexism or any other oppressions in isolation from each other, it has quickly become clear that such notions are over-simplistic and, indeed, can be oppressive in themselves. As Morris argues,

> It is not very helpful to talk about disabled women experiencing a 'double disadvantage'. Images of disadvantage are such an important part of the experience of oppression that emancipatory research (research which seeks to further the interests of 'the researched') must consistently challenge them. Therein lies one of the problems with examining the relationship between gender and disability, race and disability in terms of 'double disadvantage'. The research can itself become part of the oppression.
>
> (Morris 1992, p. 162)

Further, such additive approaches have also been criticised by black disabled people who argue that their experience of disability can only be understood within the context of racism. Thus according to one black researcher,

> In my opinion, the concept of double discrimination, as propagated by white disabled feminists is an inadequate framework within which to understand racism within disability . . . on the contrary, I suggest that racism within disability is part

of a process of simultaneous oppression which black people experience daily in Western society.

(Stuart 1992, p. 179)

Whether simultaneous oppression offers a more adequate way of understanding disability is something that only further, more developed emancipatory research can show. But certainly people are beginning to talk about their experience in this way.

As a black disabled woman, I cannot compartmentalise or separate aspects of my identity in this way. The collective experience of my race, disability and gender are what shape and inform my life.

(Hill 1994, p. 7)

Whether such a concept can cope with old, black, gay, disabled people remains an open question. So too do its links with middle range theorising and grand theory. Such questions indicate that, after ten years, our work is only just beginning – I hope we have begun to address some of the right questions even if we haven't found any of the right answers. But answers to these questions are essential if we are to provide enabling services.

It is a misuse of resources to provide me with personal assistants who are unable to cope with my sexuality...I now state at the outset that I live with my lesbian lover. If they accept it I expect respect for myself, my partner and our children. The recognition of identity and difference are the key to the success or failure of service provision.

(Gillespie-Sells 1994, p. 7)

So the argument has come full circle. If the category disability is to be produced in ways different from the individualised, pathological way it is currently produced, then what should be researched is not the disabled people of the positivist and interpretive research paradigms but the disablism ingrained in the individualistic consciousness and institutionalised practices of what is, ultimately, a disablist society.

## Conclusions

This chapter has suggested that understanding societal responses to long-term disability is no simple task and requires us to analyse ourselves and the discourses we use in order to talk about our world. It has argued that disability is produced as a social category and that in order to understand disability production we must develop a materialist discourse. Such a discourse involves a re-evaluation of our ontological, epistemological and methodological assumptions about disability. Finally, and central to this re-evaluation, we can only comprehend, challenge and change the hegemony that is disability by understanding the inter-relations between these ontological, epistemological and methodological levels.

Just as we can produce red cars or blue cars or black cars, or cars with three, four or six wheels, or hamburgers made with beef, or ham, or soya beans, so too with disability. We do not have to continue to produce disability as individual pathology and a welfare problem. We can produce it in other forms – do we want to?

# 10
# Disability, Politics and Citizenship

## Introduction

This chapter will return to the relationship between the personal and political, originally discussed in Chapter 1. Its main focus will be on collective empowerment and this will be discussed in relation to the rise of the disability movement in Britain. The discussion will draw upon the recent reintroduction of the idea of citizenship, heralded by the publication of the Citizen's Charter. It will also attempt to deal with some of the rejoinders that have been made since I originally published my claim that the disability movement was a political movement with more in common with the newly emerging social movements than either corporatist interest group politics or humanitarian, charitable and voluntary organisation responses.

What is interesting about the reintroduction of the idea of citizenship is that it offers us a way of speaking out the relationship between individuals and the State at times when this relationship is in crisis. As I suggested earlier, three times in

145

the last 150 years we have seen such crises and the emergence of citizenship as a way of talking about it. In the middle of the nineteenth century this crisis was resolved by the development of political suffrage. After the Second World War the crisis was resolved by the establishment of the universal welfare state. How the current crisis will be resolved is a matter for conjecture, but it seems clear that social movements and among them, the disability movement, will have a key role to play. Hence the focus of this chapter.

## Empowerment – the political is the personal

In considering the process and politics of empowerment, the links with citizenship should be noted, along with its connection to a central concern with the relationship of individuals to society:

> Citizenship, as equal participation in a national community, is one means of achieving social and political integration, either through the general acceptance of common values or through the negation of divisive inequalities.
>
> (Barbalet 1988, p. 81)

However, Barbalet goes on to point out that citizenship should not be regarded only as a force for the integration of individuals into society.

To do so would be to ignore the fact that citizenship has sometimes been a focus for social conflict as well as social harmony. The idea of citizenship has been an exclusive one as well as an inclusive one. Certainly, as far as disabled people are concerned, we seem to have been excluded from the Citizen's Charter and, by implication, from both the responsibilities and entitlements of citizenship.

Before considering this further I need to make explicit my own basic assumption about the relationship between the individual and society. This stands in direct opposition to Mrs Thatcher's oft quoted view that there is no such thing as society, only individuals. My own view is that we are only social beings; without society we cannot exist. In stating this position, I draw on an older and much more important authority.

Though man is a unique individual – and it is just his particularity which makes him an individual, a really individual social being – he is equally the whole, the subjective existence of society as thought and experienced. He exists in reality, as the representation and real mind of social existence, and as the sum of human manifestation of life.

(Marx in Bottomore and Rubel 1971, p. 92)

This is not to deny that there are individual as well as collective aspects to the process of empowerment. Indeed, some would insist that individual impairment is the key to collective empowerment. 'The key to understanding empowerment is an understanding of the notion of self-empowerment' (Fenton 1989, p. 42). My argument would reverse this emphasis and suggest that the key to understanding self-empowerment is the notion of collective empowerment and I shall go on to discuss collective empowerment shortly.

It is often assumed that empowerment is a process by which those in society who have power can dispense some of this to those who don't have any. This underpins many recent social policy developments where it is assumed that professionals through the development of appropriate practices can empower their clients. Central to this notion is a discourse which renames clients as 'users' or 'consumers'; supposedly empowering. Not only that, but the process of empowerment somehow becomes objectified as a thing; what's more a thing that can be delivered by those who have it to those who don't.

A study which encapsulates this view was published recently and contains a section entitled 'Managing for Empowerment'. It further states the beliefs of its authors:

We have believed since our original study of social service teams in the 1970s that the person with most influence upon the service which the user receives is the first line manager. *He or she thus plays a vital role in user and carer empowerment.* [My emphasis]

(Stevenson and Parsloe 1993, p. 12)

Empowerment is not like that however; it is a collective process on which the powerless embark as part of the struggle to resist the oppression of others, as part of their demands to be included, and/or to articulate their own views of the world.

Central to this struggle is the recognition by the powerless that they are oppressed; first articulated in respect of disability by the Union of the Physically Impaired Against Segregation in the 1970s and more recently been given a theoretical re-formulation within 'oppression theory' more generally (Abberley 1987).

Collective empowerment then becomes the process by which groups begin to struggle against this recognised oppression as the writings of people like Freire (1972) and Biko (1978) graphically demonstrate in respect of South America and South Africa and the early writing of Sutherland (1981) describes in respect of disability. So what will be described here is the process of collective empowerment that disabled people have embarked upon in Britain.

## Collective empowerment and disabled people

For present purposes we can consider that the process of the collective empowerment of disabled people began in the 1960s although blind people had begun the process decades earlier (Pagel 1988). While this process continued in the 1970s, it was the decade of the 1980s that has seen a transformation in our understandings of the nature of disability, and consequently the kinds of policies and services necessary to ensure the full economic and social integration of disabled people, as required by the United Nations Declaration of the Rights of Disabled Persons, formally adopted in 1975.

At the heart of this transformation has been the rise in the number of organisations controlled and run by disabled people themselves. At the beginning of the decade there were very few such organisations but by 1990 there was an international organisation known as Disabled Peoples International (DPI), a national co-ordinating body, the British Council of Organisations of Disabled People (BCODP) had been formed, and its constituent organisations had risen to over ninety, most of whom were local coalitions of disabled people or centres for integrated living (CILs).

The process of collective empowerment is not something that only disabled people are undergoing. In the late twentieth century, economic and technological changes, social disorganisation, changing patterns of family life and ecological crises, have led to feelings of disenfranchisement more generally. This is beginning to have an influence on the political system with the emergence of many new groups of all kinds; environmentalists, pacifists, the unemployed, welfare recipients, minority groups and the like. A number of social theorists have called these groups 'new social movements' (Touraine 1981; Boggs 1986).

In earlier writings (Oliver and Zarb 1989; Oliver 1990), I argued that the formation of these organisations controlled and run by disabled people constituted a movement, and that collectively, these organisations exhibited the characteristics of new social movements. In a recent paper disabled activist Ken Davis (1993) not only describes the history of what he calls 'the disability movement' but he claims that this movement constitutes what social theorists would call a new social movement.

Whether or not the disability movement constitutes a new social movement is an issue to which we shall return shortly, but by any standards its numerical growth was remarkable. There are three reasons why it was even more remarkable than appears at first sight. Firstly, all organisations controlled by disabled people suffered from chronic underfunding throughout the decade, even from national and international agencies which are supposed to support such developments but who continue to channel most of their funds to non-accountable, non-representative organisations.

Secondly, many politicians, policy makers and professionals were, and remain, suspicious of the viability of a new movement which was being built by a group who had seemed passive and dependent. Thirdly, the new movement was built in the teeth of opposition from the traditional voluntary organisations who, up to now, had been in control of disability and who still receive ten times more funding from the government each year than do organisations controlled by disabled people themselves.

Having described some of the difficulties, it is important not to get carried away by euphoria and fail to subject the disability movement to critical analysis. Critics often focus on the representative nature of this disability movement and accuse it of not speaking for all disabled people. This is certainly true but then no representative organisations represent all of their constituency.

In representative democracies, representation is always less than perfect. For example, the Conservative Party does not represent all conservative voters nor does the British Medical Association represent all doctors. No one would dream of denying the claims of the Conservative Party to represent conservatives nor the BMA to represent the views of doctors. And yet the right of the disability movement to represent disabled people is continually questioned, by politicians, policy makers and professionals alike.

This point is developed by Altman (1989) in making a distinction between what he calls 'movement' and 'community'. He develops this further in the context of gay politics:

> We can think of the gay world as consisting of a number of concentric circles: at the centre are those people who openly identify as gays, and whose social and communal activities exist largely within a gay milieu. Then there are those who are openly gay, but not in all areas of their work and social life. Then there are those who accept themselves as homosexual but do not feel part of a larger gay community as a result. Lastly there are very many people who are behaviourally homosexual but do not consider this as part of their identity. The gay movement will draw almost exclusively from the first two categories, but these are themselves in part the product of the movement. Both identity, and conscious affiliation to the gay community, are processes which change over time in an individual's life.
>
> (Altman 1989, pp. 47–8)

This distinction between movement and community is a useful one in considering the politics of disability. Certainly it would be true to say that not all of the six million disabled people in Britain see themselves as part of a disability community, let alone as supporters of the aims or the tactics of the movement. What is true however is that issues that the movement has placed on the political agenda such as rights, access, choice and control are issues relevant to the wider community.

What is also true, as will be returned to later, is that increasing numbers of disabled people within the community are identifying with and joining the movement. And what is undeniable is that if the legitimate claims of the movement to represent the interests of disabled people are denied, who else will represent our interests – doctors? politicians? the Royal Institutes and Associations?

Where it is perhaps more legitimate to ask questions about representation is in the context of other oppressed groups. Hence Hill (1992) criticises the disability movement for not fully involving black disabled people and their newly emerging organisations and Morris (1991) makes similar criticisms in respect of disabled women.

Kirsten Hearn provides a poignant account of how disabled lesbians and gay men are excluded from all their potential communities. 'The severely able-bodied community and straight disabled community virtually ignored our campaign' (Hearn 1991, p. 30). 'Issues of equality are not fashionable for the majority of the severely able-bodied, white, middle-class lesbian and gay communities' (Hearn 1991, p. 33). In response to this 'multiple oppression' alongside existing organisations, disabled lesbians and gay men have set up newer organised groups geared towards collective empowerment. These include LANGUID (Lesbians And Gays United In Disability) and REGARD to 'combat the homophobia of the disability movement' (Hearn 1991).

While these criticisms are undoubtedly fair, the disability movement exists in a society which institutionalises racism, sexism, homophobia and disablism. The movement should be judged by the way it struggles against these oppressions, not by their eradication. All institutions and organisations are bound to reproduce oppression while oppression remains a feature of society. Oppression can only be totally eradicated from organisations when it is eradicated from society and it will only be eradicated from society as part of our struggles to eradicate it from our organisations. And it should be remembered that many of the more traditional voluntary organisations and even some statutory service providers do not even acknowledge that such issues exist (Connelly 1988, 1990).

While it would be easy to be complacent, it is true that the disability movement has made significant progress in trying to include a range of oppressions. Hasler (1993), in discussing some of these issues faced by the disability movement in the last ten years, is optimistic in suggesting a more satisfactory incorporation of them into the movement in the future.

A sign of health for the disability movement is perhaps the number of groups still emerging to represent new interest groups.

(Hasler 1993, p. 283)

To return to the remarkable growth of the disability movement; it needs to be emphasised that this was not merely a numerical phenomenon, but also reflected the individual and collective empowerment of disabled people through the organisations they were creating. This individual and collective empowerment can be seen in a number of ways.

It can be seen in the challenge to dominant social perceptions of disability as personal tragedy and the affirmation of positive images of disability through the development of a politics of personal identity. It can also be seen in the development and articulation of the social model of disability which both provided a critique of the existing individual model and the basis for more appropriate service provision and professional practice.

It can further be seen through the development of a disability culture and the public affirmation of this through the disability arts movement. Finally it can be seen in the collective self-confidence of disabled people to engage in their own political activities and no longer to be reliant on traditional forms of political articulation through the party system or single issue pressure groups (Oliver and Zarb 1989).

## The struggle for citizenship

All this can be seen as part of a broader struggle by disabled people; to be included in, rather than excluded from, society. In other words, to be accepted as citizens with all that entails in terms of rights and responsibilities. Central to this has been the concerted campaign for anti-discrimination legislation and it is possible to identify three key influences on the demands for legislation to outlaw discrimination against disabled people in Britain. While it is possible to treat all these influences as analytically distinct, they are interconnected and have all affected each other and played a significant role in the current demands.

The first of these influences was the Civil Rights Movement in the United States which focused around the struggles of black people in the 1950s to achieve basic rights to vote, to hold elective office and the right to be tried by a jury of one's peers. As these rights were gradually achieved, the Movement became concerned with social rights generally and had an influence on other groups such as women and disabled people.

There were two aspects to this influence; a reconceptualisation of the unequal treatment of such groups as a human rights issue and a realisation of the possibilities of achieving social change.

As one commentator has put it:

> The Civil Rights Movement has had an effect not only on the securing of certain rights but also on the manner in which those rights have been secured. When traditional legal channels have been exhausted, disabled persons have learned to employ other techniques of social protest, such as demonstrations and sit-ins.
>
> (De Jong 1983, p. 12)

These techniques of social protest stood disabled Americans in good stead when forcing Section 504 of the Rehabilitation Act (1973) onto the statute books against a backsliding Government and more recently, played no small part in the passage of the Americans with Disabilities Act (1990); both of which effectively address the issue of institutional discrimination against disabled people in the USA.

A second factor which has influenced the demand for anti-discrimination legislation has been the passage of similar acts to outlaw discrimination on the grounds of race and gender in this country. Early attempts at legislation in these areas had proved ineffective but both the Sex Discrimination Act (1975) and the Race Relations Act (1976) had an influence on the demands of disabled people for similar legislation. There were two reasons for this; to begin with the passing of such legislation acknowledged the existence of discrimination and made it clear that it was unacceptable; and in addition, both Acts attempted to deal with indirect as well as direct discrimination. Disabled people, therefore, want similar treatment to other groups before the law and also legal recognition of the fact that discrimination is more than just the intentional acts of prejudiced individuals.

Unlike women and black people, however, the principle of equality for disabled people has never been enshrined in the law. This is a clear indication of both the lack of acknowledgement of the existence of discrimination against disabled people and the lack of importance attached to notions of equal opportunities. In addition this lack of acknowledgement of the

existence of discrimination against disabled people fails to recognise the way discrimination is compounded for disabled
members of the gay community, black people and women with
impairments (Campling 1981; Conference of Indian Organisations 1987; Lesbian and Gay Committee 1990; Lonsdale 1990,
Morris 1989).

A third factor which had an influence on the demand for
anti-discrimination legislation was the coming together of individual disabled people to form their own organisations (Oliver
and Zarb 1989; Oliver 1990). Not only did this foster a growing collective consciousness amongst disabled people but also
a reformulation of what the problems of disability actually were,
shifting the focus squarely away from the functional limitations
of impaired individuals and onto contemporary social organisation, with its plethora of disabling barriers. This nascent collective organising also saw the start of a developing schism
between organisations for the disabled and organisations of
disabled people.

This schism is not unrelated to demands for anti-discrimination legislation for many of the establishment organisations
were confidently (and usually confidentially) advising the Government of the day that discrimination was not a problem for
disabled people and that therefore legislation in this area was
unnecessary. This stance was adopted despite the fact that the
Silver Jubilee Access Committee had drawn attention to a number
of 'blatant acts of discrimination against disabled people' (SJAC,
1979) and that the official committee which was set up to in-
vestigate this discrimination was unequivocal in both its recognition of the fact that discrimination against disabled people
was widespread and that anti-discrimination legislation was essential to remedy this unacceptable state of affairs (CORAD 1981).

The campaign for equal status for disabled people, spear-
headed by organisations of disabled people intensified in the
1980s and the formation of the Voluntary Organisations for
Anti-Discrimination Legislation (VOADL) Committee signified
the conversion of many of the organisations for the disabled
to the point of view articulated by disabled people themselves.
Conversion on this issue however, does not mean that the schism
between such organisations has ceased to be of significance.

Nor would it be appropriate to reduce the contribution of
the self-organisation of disabled people to that of spearhead-
ing the campaign for legal rights for they have been in the

forefront of campaigns for economic, social and political rights as well; they have attacked inappropriate service provision and professional practice and pioneered the demands from disabled people to live independently. Indeed, it was the idea of independent living which gave a focus to the struggles of disabled people to organise themselves, initially in the United States and subsequently elsewhere, including Britain (Pagel 1988).

In order to harness this growing consciousness of disabled people, to provide a platform to articulate the re-definition of the problem of disability and to give a focus to the campaigns for independent living and against discrimination, the BCODP was formed in 1981 and its success in the subsequent decade is entirely an achievement of disabled people themselves (Hasler, 1993). Its conception and subsequent development have been achieved without extensive financial support from Government or from traditional organisations for disabled people.

On the contrary, the BCODP was criticised from the start as being elitist, isolationist, unrepresentative, and Marxist by a collection of unrepresentative non-disabled people, right and left wing academics, isolated and elitist staff and management of traditional organisations and many professionals whose very careers were bound up with keeping disabled people dependent (Goodall 1988; Harrison 1987; Holden 1990; Williams 1983). Yet despite these attacks, BCODP has gone from strength to strength, now representing over 90 organisations of disabled people and 300 000 disabled individuals.

These initiatives not only established BCODP as the only representative voice of disabled people in Britain but by its very success it stimulated an ever growing number of disabled people to adopt a disabled identity. With this growing sense of a collective, political identity has developed the self-confidence not simply to ask for the necessary changes but to demand them and to use a whole range of tactics including direct action and civil disobedience. It's because of this growing collective self-confidence that disabled people are forcing the issue of institutional discrimination onto the political agenda and demanding anti-discrimination legislation to remedy it.

Thus throughout the 1980s there has been a growing campaign to persuade the British Government to introduce anti-discrimination legislation to enable disabled people to participate fully in the mainstream economic and social life of society. During the last ten years there have been thirteen attempts to get such legislation onto the statute books (Oliver 1985a; Barnes 1991). Hitherto successive governments have successfully prevented the passage of these bills, initially arguing that there is little if any widespread discrimination against disabled people and subsequently, that while discrimination may be widespread, legislation is not the way to tackle the problem. Indeed a former Minister for Disabled People shifted his own personal position in exactly the way described above.

Seeing the problems that disabled people face as the result of discrimination, has led some parts of the disability movement to adopt some of the tactics of the civil rights movement two decades earlier in the United States, taking direct action to confront the pedestrianisation of some city centres, to insist that transport systems which force a form of apartheid on more than a million people with mobility impairments cannot legitimately claim to be public and to challenge the degrading stereotypes presented by the mass media. The success of these tactics cannot be doubted and the most significant victory came with the demise of Telethon after major demonstrations in 1990 and 1992.

The American disability movement has used such tactics to good effect in the past twenty years to the point where their most recent convert can claim after signing the Americans with Disabilities Act 1990 which outlawed discrimination 'Let the shameful walls of exclusion come tumbling down' (President Bush 1990). It would be nice to think that the ex-Minister for Disabled People will suffer a similar conversion but his current equivocating does not make this seem likely. 'I am not sure whether blanket anti-discrimination legislation . . . is the appropriate way to proceed' (Nicholas Scott 1990). Nor, it seems, is a new incumbent in the post likely to produce much change of views. Whether or not the politicians are certain that anti-discrimination legislation is the way to proceed, disabled people are, and their ever increasing self confidence and political strength makes it inevitable that such legislation will reach the statute books here as well as in the United States.

## Is the disability movement a new social movement?

In light of this analysis of the disability movement, we need to return to the claims that it constitutes a new social movement. According to theorists, these movements have four essential characteristics:

1. they remain on the margins of the political system,
2. they offer a critical evaluation of society,
3. they imply a society with different forms of valuation and distribution,
4. the issues they raise transcend national boundaries.

It is certainly true that the disability movement exists on the margins of the political system; the single issue pressure groups such as DIG and the Disability Alliance have a closer relationship to the political parties and the State continues to provide ten times as much funding to traditional 'voluntary organisations for the disabled' than for the disability movement and this situation has changed little despite the rhetoric of user involvement which has accompanied recent legislative changes (Drake 1994).

However, increasingly representatives of the movement are playing a more active role in the formal political system, in areas like pressing for anti-discrimination legislation, in the vanguard of pressure for the government to change the law on direct payments to disabled people and so on. The fine line between marginalisation and incorporation (Oliver 1990) remains one that the movement must address; it must be close enough to the political institutions of the state to be an effective change agent but must guard against becoming an establishment organisation more concerned with OBEs for its leaders than representing the wishes of disabled people.

Secondly, the disability movement provides a critique of the oppressive structures of society in general and more specifically a challenge to the medical and professional domination of health and welfare provision. Thirdly, cultural expressions of the disability movement (Morrison and Finkelstein 1993) provide a challenge to the stigmatisation of difference in its insistence that disability is a cause for celebration. Finally, disability crosses national boundaries to focus attention on global issues such as war, poverty and industrial exploitation and the role they play in creating impairments and sustaining disability.

But to return to the theme of citizenship, one recent commentator on these new movements suggests that their central concerns are different from other kinds of political movement:

The point here is that while new movements may be distinguished from older movements because their demands are expressed in terms of autonomy rather than citizenship, etc, such notions themselves entail a whole range of political questions and demands.

(Scott 1990, p. 23)

While it is certainly true that a major plank of the disability movement has been autonomy conceptualised as independence and that this has been given a central focus by centres for independent living; nonetheless, the rights of citizenship are certainly seen as crucial to the wishes of disabled people to live independently.

Scott himself concedes this point in terms of his general analysis of new social movements:

Furthermore, some aspects of new social movement ideology are quite clearly concerned with existing political institutions, and can very well be understood in terms of citizenship, representation and so on. This is especially so with regard to a second class of new social movement aims, namely, those concerned with 'citizens rights', that is, with acquiring for some section of the population those rights which are ascribed to the average citizen, and from which particular groups are systematically excluded.

(Scott 1990, p. 23)

Certainly it is true that disabled people have been systematically excluded from British society; they have been denied inclusion into their society because of the existence of disabling barriers.

Not all would accept the idea that the disability movement is a new social movement. Shakespeare (1993) distinguishes between post-materialist and liberation movements and argues that the disability movement belongs in the latter category. Thus the movement is not about post-material values but resource allocation:

Most of the struggles mentioned above are about resource allocation: women, black people and disabled people are crucially concerned with their economic exploitation and poverty.

(Shakespeare 1993, p. 258)

Of course they are, but their struggles for liberation recognise that it is not merely the mechanics of resource allocation that must change, but the values on which such allocations are based. And it is clear that resources are currently allocated on the basis of materialist values; therefore if they are to change, they will need to be based on a different set of values – post materialist, if you like.

An attempt has been made to relate the debate about new social movements to relative or universal definitions of human need. Hewitt is critical of what he sees as post-modernist theories of social movements in that they emphasise relative needs and particularistic interests and, instead that we should move to the position where 'Universal needs emerge contingently in the dialogue between social movements representing groups in need, and the wider public and policy makers' (Hewitt 1993, p. 72). While this may become true in the future, the political reality at present is that particularistic social movements cannot rely on universalistic political processes. Disabled people know from the lessons of their own history (in part re-produced in Chapter 2) that universalistic politics will fail them as it has in the past. Linking the campaign for a national disability income to broad left politics and the mobilisation of public support not only failed to deliver the solution, it incorrectly identified the problem (UPIAS 1976).

Thus, for me, the disability movement, is a new social movement, and is beginning to offer disabled people a political voice; something they never had before. In similar ways, other new social movements are offering other disenfranchised groups a voice where they previously didn't have one.

The significance of this for the existing political system remains an open question but it is clear that traditional forms of democratic representation are coming under increasing pressure. It is becoming apparent that representative democracy in the twentieth century was a game played largely by white, middle-class men and the crisis between individuals and the State will only be resolved by broadening the representativeness of our political institutions. In this, new social movements may have a crucial role to play.

As I have argued, this denial of inclusion into the political process constitutes a denial of citizenship for disabled people. Thus it is not surprising that these new social movements in general and the disability movement in particular are concerned with forcing governments to accord their constituents the social, political and civil rights of citizenship currently denied to them:

Civil rights movements, or those aspects of social movements concerned with civil rights, are clearly oriented towards central political institutions, particularly towards governments and the legal system. They demand a recognition on the part of society to formal and substantive equality for sections of the population, and respect for the rights of members of those sections to equal treatment not as individuals but as citizens.

(Scott 1990, p. 24)

Thus it is no accident that a major initiative stemming from the disability movement at this time is the demand for anti-discrimination legislation (Barnes 1991). According to Oliver and Barnes (1991), discrimination is so deeply embedded in all aspects of social organisation and social structure, including our welfare services that it is effectively institutionalised.

While ADL would not eradicate it overnight it would send a clear message to society that discrimination was unacceptable. In addition it would give disabled people similar rights not to experience discrimination as are currently given to women and black people. Finally, it would force change on existing welfare institutions. However, ADL in itself is not enough to ensure for disabled people full social, political and civil rights. There are other things that need to change; other barriers that need to be removed than simply those of discrimination.

There are a number of dangers that the disability movement needs to guard against when anti-discrimination legislation comes, as it undoubtedly will. Firstly, it must be seen as a means, not an end; it must be seen as a platform for the continuing struggle for citizenship, not as a sign that citizenship has been achieved. The American movement some twenty years ago, saw the signing of Section 504 as an end, and as a consequence, when it was signed, the power of the movement declined rather than increased (Scotch 1984).

Secondly, the British legislation, when it comes, will undoubtedly provide a 'disability commission' to police and monitor the legislation. The commission will probably have a token disabled person appointed to spearhead it and it will become an exercise in the management and containment of disability politics rather than an enforcement agency. Certainly that is the fate that has befallen the commissions designed to enforce anti-discrimination legislation in the areas of race and gender.

While the rush to a legislation approach, characteristic of the

United States, might turn out to be counterproductive, proper enforcement will be essential to achieving citizenship. The rational way to ensure such enforcement would be to properly resource a representative and accountable organisation like BCODP to do the job. Control of the process of enforcement would then neither be in the hands of the establishment nor the legal mafia. Such a strategy would also serve a broader purpose in opening up our political institutions to wider representation and give one new social movement an enhanced role in politics.

## Conclusion

In discussing citizenship in this chapter, I have concentrated on attempts to obtain the rights and entitlements of citizenship. The responsibilities and duties of citizenship are also relevant to collective empowerment. Empowered groups whose rights and responsibilities are constantly denied by a non-responsive formal political system, may seek to develop informal and more direct forms of political expression and activity.

Historically we have seen examples of this with the American Civil Rights Movement and more recently disabled people in the United States have undertaken sit-ins to ensure the passage of anti-discrimination legislation onto the statute books. The disability movement in this country, as well as continuing to articulate its demands through formal political channels, has also participated in mass marches and rallies to protest about cuts in the benefits systems, held demonstrations against the presentation of charitable images of disability on television, and embarked upon campaigns of civil disobedience in protest against inaccessible public transport systems and the pedestrianisation of some inner city shopping areas.

Once people begin to empower themselves, there can be no turning back; the world can never be the same again. The challenge for the twenty-first century is whether our economic, social and political institutions can adapt to accommodate to the demands of empowered people, or returning to the theme of citizenship, active citizens. The answer is beyond the scope of this book so the final chapter will attempt to pull together the themes discussed so far.

# 11
# Intellectuals and the Disability Movement

## Introduction

This final chapter is completely new and is an attempt to make sense of my own experience in, and relationship to, the disability movement. It is neither a statement of what I think my position in this relationship is or should be but an attempt to open up the issue of the role of individuals in collective movements. In discussing this, I use the word intellectual not in the bourgeois sense of the term but to describe all individuals who think critically about their lives. Not all disabled people do of course: some think the only problem is non-disabled people; some think the problems they face are their own fault; some think disabled people should accept the hand-outs they are given and be grateful. What unites disabled people within the movement is that not only do we think our lives could be better, we know they should be. Intellectual work is but one path to achieving the social transformation necessary to make it so.

## The personal may be the political

Earlier I alluded to the suspicion that the disability movement has had towards individuals who might sell the movement down the river. This suspicion has extended to those individuals who might be called intellectuals and has, at times, bordered on anti-intellectualism. Political and social movements of all kinds have been suspicious of the role of intellectuals in developing theory as the following quote in respect of feminism suggests:

> In a society where theorising has been the province of men, and where their theories have so often been used to mystify, to intimidate and to oppress, it is well that we as women should be wary of what we have come to see as theory – and theorists. We have witnessed elites using their power to justify their position: from the rich we have heard that the poor are responsible for their own poverty, from the whites that blacks have only themselves to blame for their depressed position in society, and from men that women are content with their lot and choose their subordination.
>
> (Spender 1982, p. 16)

To that could be added that disabled people can only expect to be second class citizens because of the tragedy of their impairments.

The relationship between the individual and the collective is an issue for all political and social movements, as is the question of the relationship between the processes of individual and collective empowerment. This leads to the crux of political life itself; the relationship between individual and social action. These are the themes that will be addressed in this chapter in the context of my own participation in the disability movement. This participation has been both as an intellectual developing theory about disability and also as an activist involved in the full range of political activity from lobbying to direct action. However, I should add that while, conceptually, it is possible to separate out these two areas of my life, in reality, they are inextricably linked.

Earlier I described how my own political consciousness was kick-started by listening to the music of Bob Dylan. Within the disability movement a number of disabled artists and performers have emerged to write and sing about the experience of disability.

One of these, Ian Stanton was led to critically reflect on his own relationship to the disability movement:

> there is unquestionably a degree of suspicion of 'disability arts'. 'Art' is unaccountable, and disabled people have a long history of having unaccountable individuals – both disabled and non-disabled – speaking on our behalf.
>
> Perhaps there's something in this – art is essentially a personal expression (if other people like it, so much the better) and how can personal feelings be 'accountable'? You can't produce a painting or a song by discussing it in a committee.
>
> (Stanton 1991, pp. 20–1)

While this is, of course, true in one sense of the word, art emerges out of experience, both individual and collective. And, as Stanton notes in his article, collective oppression has been the driving force of much artistic expression, although he puts it slightly differently. '"Art" has recorded every civil rights victory, every form of brutality, every oppression, every emotion of humankind' (Stanton 1991, p. 20). My own individual relationship to the disability movement has led me to similar reflections. How much are my own writings the product of the intellectual work of an unaccountable individual and how much are they reflective of the collective experience of oppression? The question is a rhetorical one but leads to a further one concerning the relationship of individuals to social movements. Often intellectuals are accused, and in many cases rightly, of joining movements for their own careerist reasons:

> feminist and minority intellectuals are drawn to movements whose actions may well have helped them gain entry into academic work; their problems have to do less with whether participation is possible than with how to define roles that make use of their training, skills and position and how to overcome their marginality.
>
> (Flacks 1991, p. 15)

However, while in some movements, intellectuals may be in marginal positions, that is not the case as far as the disability movement is concerned. Having an impairment makes it much harder for intellectuals to deny or move beyond the roots of their experience. In my own terms, I can never move beyond my impairment because getting up and going to bed every day still has to be arranged and negotiated (and even paid for) and will remain so for the rest of my life.

That is not to say that some disabled people may move beyond their impairments in the same way as other social movements have found their leaders moving beyond their experiential base in terms of gender, race or sexual orientation giving rise to what has been called the uncle Tom and the tiny Tim syndrome. Often such actions are seen as 'selling out' although not everyone is content to dismiss such activity as nothing more than collaboration:

> Those disabled people who ally themselves with organisations for disabled people do so predominantly because their class position leads them to fear radical change. Some of us may feel a sense of outrage at how such disabled people are used to give legitimacy to the organisations which do so much to oppress disabled people. We must also recognise, however, that internalised oppression exerts a tremendous influence. A disabled person who holds a position within a conservative charitable organisation has been told all their lives – as we all have – how inadequate and pitiable disabled people are. Small wonder then that such people, when asked to involve more disabled people in their organisation, commonly respond that there isn't any capable person with the relevant expertise amongst the disabled community.
>
> (Morris 1991, p. 177)

This relationship between disabled individuals and the disability movement has a wider dimension as well; I have already discussed in Chapter 5 the discovery of the 'user' who must be consulted about service provision. Often this smacks as little more than tokenism as one study recently discovered:

> We have a whole group of hand-picked users who go to user meetings – hand-picked by social services – and then we're told that social services is consulting with users.
>
> (quoted in Bewley and Glendinning 1994)

The only solution to this is the recognition that only democratic and accountable organisations of disabled people should be asked to speak for disabled people.

## The personal must be the political

When organisations emerge out the reinterpretation of personal experience as political, as is the case with the feminist movement, black struggles and the disability movement, then the tension between individuals and the collectivity becomes a crucial issue. It is a tension between the organisation becoming bureaucratic and oligarchical and remaining democratic and rooted in the personal experiences of its membership. This tension is particularly acute in respect of new social movements because seeing the end of the separation between personal and public spheres is central to their world views.

One problem of course, is that as social movements become more successful, so the leadership become more prominent and

'Prominent personalities' are seen to have a destructive effect on the attempt by the movements to create credible alternatives to prevailing political structures. The usefulness of intellectual inspirers is questioned by activists who draw the distinction between the capacity of such people to generate publicity for the movement and the practical skills required by militants engaged in a locally based social struggle.

(Papadakis 1993, p. 90)

The issue of prominent personalities was one of the major bones of contention between UPIAS and the Disability Alliance, documented in Chapter 2. The Alliance wanted a small group of expert 'intellectuals' to speak on behalf of disabled people which is, in itself, a threat to the disability movement, as Finkelstein has recently argued:

I regarded it as important to draw attention to this as a potential threat to the movement. This was because any strategy which gave credibility to a single issue approach, such as the incomes approach, could divert the energy and attention of disabled people away from the task of organisation building into the dead end of supporting the experts as they write about and present their arguments for the rank and file.

(Finkelstein 1994)

The tension between ideas and action emerges yet again; the tension between intellectuals whose role is to create theory and political activists whose role is to produce social change. Such a tension can be resolved however in movements where theory emerges not from marginal intellectuals but from those struggles that are born out of personal experience as with feminism, for example:

> Feminist theory owes its existence to the struggles of those who did not have as their goal the creation of theory. That is, feminist theory is intimately tied to a political movement conceived as a struggle for liberation. This connection with the idea of liberation as carried forth by self-reflective, embodied human being accounts for the meaningfulness and insightfulness of feminist theory as well as its creative, critical and compelling nature.
>
> (Wallach Ballogh 1991, p. 31)

Crucial to this is the distinction between what Gramsci called structural or positional intellectuals, and organic intellectuals. In making this distinction, Gramsci was discussing the issue in respect of working class movements where the development and control of ideas often seemed to be in the control of middle-class individuals, hence raising questions about the relationship of personal experience to social theory.

Having an impairment makes it difficult, though not impossible, to be anything other than an organic intellectual within the disability movement. Thus while Bob Dylan might have been a positional intellectual within the civil rights movement (a white middle-class male making a good living championing the cause of the poor, the down-trodden and the oppressed), Ian Stanton and myself are organic intellectuals within the disability movement (although still making a good living by writing about the collective experience of disability in our own individual ways).

In developing this distinction, I am not seeking to make value judgements about the quality of intellectual work individuals produce nor their motives for doing it. What I am trying to say (and I would, wouldn't I?) is that social movements have less to fear from organic intellectuals than they do from positional ones. Organic intellectuals are less likely to distort the collective experience of oppression and are less likely to sell out to the highest bidder precisely because intellectual work is rooted in personal and collective experience. But that does not mean that there are no 'tiny Tim' organic intellectuals nor that all positional ones will sell the movement down the river as soon as the price is right.

The argument I am making here should not be taken to its logical conclusion. I am not suggesting that those people who have no direct experience of impairment have no contribution to make to the disability movement. After all, Karl Marx and Frederich Engels were both middle-class intellectuals who made crucial and long lasting contributions to working class movements both in their descriptions of experience (Engels 1844) and their development of transformative social theory (Marx and Engels 1967).

Within the disability movement, there has been some discussion of the role of people without impairments (or people with abilities as Vic Finkelstein has, somewhat ironically, begun to call them). This has usually centred on the role of 'allies' within the movement and crucial to this, the ability to identify who is, and who is not, an ally. Holdsworth, while admitting there is a role for allies within the movement, takes a fairly trenchant view of who they might be:

> Disabled people, for our sins, encounter a whole range of people throughout our lives; parents, carers, brothers, sisters, professionals like doctors, nurses, OT's, social workers – even celebrities who sometimes 'adopt us'. Are they our allies? Many will think so and some will be surprised to find out that, not only are they not our allies, but, in fact, are the beast itself.
>
> (Holdsworth 1993, p. 4)

Not all in the movement would accept such a position, arguing that the experience of different impairments may well be different as well as the fact that simultaneous oppression is also experienced differentially by individual disabled people. Hence the able-bodied disabled dichotomy is too simple. Shakespeare also argues, echoing earlier UPIAS discussions, that it is society, not individuals who are the real enemy:

> Our real enemy is not individuals, but the system which divides us, which creates our disability, which makes it possible for others to profit from our exclusion: it's convenient and easy to highlight people, but the focus of our rage and our action should be the structures.
>
> (Shakespeare 1993, p. 32)

Neither of these positions is in itself adequate and remind me of my days as an undergraduate sociologist when we argued about the relationship between the individual and the social, between structure and action; an argument which, incidentally, sociology itself has yet to resolve. And further, the issue is not simply one of the disability movement forging relationships with allies, but also one of creating alliances with other new social movements.

Some such alliances are beginning to be forged out of social action and political activity and this will inevitably continue. There is a series of intellectual tasks to perform in this as well; to describe and analyse the experiences of alliance creation; to identify common interests and irresolvable differences between movements and to provide visions of the future which will resolve all this. However this is intellectual work with which to begin, not end, a book and hence a job for another time, and perhaps, another person.

## Conclusion

There is no satisfactory way to conclude what is a journey that may never end. I am tempted to use the metaphor of trying to disembark from a moving train but as most of us can't get on trains in the first place, it hardly seems appropriate. The whole of what has gone before can be read as my own personal struggle to give meaning to my own life and, of course, this is indeed partly true. But I hope it is more than that. I hope it is also part of a continuing process of understanding and transforming disability; a process in which many of us are engaged and one which will continue long after this book has disappeared.

In trying to accomplish this, I am struck by the warning Foucault sounded to all who would be intellectuals, in what may have been his final interview:

The role of the intellectual does not consist in telling others what they must do. What right would they have to do that? And remember all prophecies, promises, injunctions, and programs that the intellectuals have managed to formulate in the course of the last two centuries. The job of an intellectual does not consist in moulding the political will of others. It is a matter of performing analyses in his or her own fields, of interrogating anew the evidence and postulates, of shaking up habits, ways of acting and thinking, of dispelling commonplace beliefs, of taking a new measure of rules and institutions ... it is a matter of participating in the formation of a political will, where [the intellectual] is called to perform a role as citizen.

(Foucault 1991, pp. 11–12)

Part of that role as citizen, as the authors of the Communist Manifesto knew only too well, is to connect the personal to the political, is to teach everyone about the connections between the local and the global, to illuminate the interweaving of sectional and societal interests. 'Thought and being are indeed distinct, but they also form a unity' (quoted in Bottomore and Rubel 1963, p. 93). Such a task was undertaken by those people with impairments who produced the Fundamental Principles of Disability while struggling to achieve their own individual and collective liberation. Such a project provides the criteria against which I would ask you to judge this description of my own intellectual journey.

# Bibliography

Abberley, P. (1987) 'The Concept of Oppression and the Development of a Social Theory of Disability', *Disability, Handicap and Society*, vol. 2, no. 1, 5–19.

Abberley, P. (1991) 'The Significance of the OPCS Disability Surveys', in Oliver, M. (ed.), *Social Work: Disabled People and Disabling Environments* (London: Jessica Kingsley Publishers).

Abercrombie, N., Hill, S. and Turner, B. (1988) *The Penguin Dictionary of Sociology* (London: Penguin).

Albrecht, G. (1992) *The Disability Business* (London: Sage).

Altman, D. (1989) 'The Emergence of Gay Identity in the USA and Australia' in Jennett, C. and Stewart, R. *Politics of the Future: the Role of Social Movements* (The Macmillan Company of Australia).

Audit Commission (1986) *Making a Reality of Community Care* (London: HMSO).

Audit Commission (1992a) *Getting in on the Act: Provision for Pupils with Special Educational Needs: The National Picture* (London: HMSO).

Audit Commission (1992b) *Getting the Act Together: Provision for Pupils with Special Educational Needs* (London: HMSO).

Baird, V. (1992) 'Difference or Defiance', *New Internationalist* no. 293, July.

Banyard, P. (1991) 'Research Director's Report', *ISRT Newsletter* no. 23.

Barbalet, R. (1988) *Citizenship* (Milton Keynes: Open University Press).

Barnes, C. (1990) *Cabbage Syndrome: The Social Construction of Dependency* (London: Falmer Press).

Barnes, C. (1991) *Disabled People in Britain and Discrimination* (London: Hurst & Co.).

Barnes, C. (1992) *Disabling Imagery and the Media: An Exploration of the Principles for Media Representation of Disabled People* (Ryburn Publishing and BCODP).

Barton, L. (1989a) (ed.), *Disability and Dependency* (London: Falmer Press).

Barton, L. (1989b) (ed.), *Integration: Myth or Reality* (London: Falmer Press).

Barton, L. (1993) 'Labels, Markets and Inclusive Education' in Visser, J. and Upton, G. *Special Education in Britain After Warnock* (London: David Fulton Publishers).

Barton, L. and Corbett, J. (1990) 'Transition to Adult Life; Rhetoric or Reality', Paper presented at the International Conference on Integration, Stockholm, Sweden.

Barton, L. and Tomlinson, S. (eds) (1984) *Special Education and Social Interests* (London: Methuen).

Beardshaw, V. (1988) *Last on the List: Community Services for People with Physical Disabilities* (London: King's Fund Institute).

Beresford, P. *Community Care*, 26 March 1992.

Berthoud, R. Lakey, J. and McKay, S. *The Economic Problems of Disabled People* (London: Policy Studies Institute).

Bewley, C. and Glendinning, C. (1992) *Involving Disabled People in Community Care Planning* (York: Joseph Rowntree Foundation).

Biko, S. (1978) *I Write What I Like* (Harmondsworth: Penguin).

Bilton, T., Bonnett, K., Jones, P., Stanworth, M., Sheard, K. and Webster, K. *Introductory Sociology* (Basingstoke: Macmillan).

Blaxter, M. (1976) *The Meaning of Disability* (London: Heinemann).

Blaxter, M. (1980) *The Meaning of Disability* (2nd edn) (London: Heinemann).

Boggs, C. (1986) *Social Movements and Political Power* (Philadelphia: Temple University Press).

Boocock, R. (1987) *Hegemony* (London: Tavistock).

Booth, T. (1993) 'Raising standards: Sticking to first principles' in Dyson, A. and Gains, C. *Rethinking Special Needs in Mainstream Schools* (London: David Fulton Publishers).

Booth, T. (1988) 'Challenging Conceptions of Integration' in Barton, L. (eds.) *The Politics of Special Educational Needs* (Sussex: Falmer Press).

Borsay, A. (1986) 'Personal Trouble or Public Issue? Towards a Model of Policy for People with Physical and Mental Disabilities', *Disability, Handicap and Society*, vol. 1, no. 2.

Borsay, A. (1986) *Disabled People in the Community* (London: Bedford Square Press).

Bottomore, T. and Rubel, M. (ed.) (1971) *Karl Marx: Selected Writings in Sociology and Social Philosophy* (Harmondsworth: Penguin Books).

Bourne, J. (1980) 'Cheerleaders and Ombudsmen: A Sociology of Race Relations in Britain', *Race and Class*, vol. XX1, no. 4.

Brearley, C. P. (1982) *Risk and Ageing* (London: RKP).

Brechin, A. and Liddiard, P. (1981) *Look at it this Way: New Approaches to Rehabilitation* (London: Hodder & Stoughton).

Brown, G. and Harris, T. (1979) *Social Origins of Depression* (London: Tavistock).

Bynoe, I., Oliver, M. and Barnes, C. (1991) *Equal Rights for Disabled People* (London: Institute for Public Policy Research).

Campbell, J. and Gillespie-Sells, C. (1991) *Disability Equality Training Trainers Guide* (London: CCETSW).

Campling, J. (1981) *Images of Ourselves* (Routledge & Kegan Paul, London).

CORAD (1982) *Report by the Committee on Restrictions against Disabled People* (London: HMSO).

CSIE (1991) *Getting in on the Act* (London: Centre for Studies on Integration in Education).

Carver, V. (1982) 'The individual behind the statistics', Unit 3 in *The Handicapped Person in the Community (Block 1)* (Milton Keynes: Open University Press).

Cashling, D. (1993) 'Cobblers and Song-birds: the language and imagery of disability', *Disability, Handicap and Society*, vol. 8, no. 2, 199–206.

Cohen, S. (1985) *Visions of Social Control* (Oxford: Polity Press).

Coleridge, P. (1993) *Disability, Liberation and Development* (Oxford: Oxfam Publications).

Connelly, N. (1988) *Care in the Multi-racial Community* (London: PSI).

Connelly, N. (1990) *Between Apathy and Outrage: Voluntary Organisations in Multi-racial Britain* (London: PSI).

Cook, J. and Mitchell, P. (1982) 'Putting teeth into the Act: A history of attempts to enforce the provisions of section 2 of the Chronically Sick and Disabled Persons Act 1970' (London: RADAR).

Coote, A. (ed.) (1992) *The Welfare of Citizens: Developing New Social Rights* (London: Rivers Oram Press).

Conrad, P. and Schneider, J. (1980) *Deviance and Medicalisation: From Badness to Sickness* (St. Louis: Mosley).

Crow, L. (1992) 'Renewing the Social Model of Disability', *Coalition*, July 1992.

DIG (1988) *Not the OPCS Survey – Being Disabled Costs more than They Said* (London: Disability Income Group).

Dalley, G. (1991) (ed.) *Disability and Social Policy* (London: Policy Studies Institute).

Daunt, P. (1991) *Meeting Disability; A European Response* (London: Cassell).

Davies, J. and Davies, P. (1989) *A Teacher's Guide to Support Services* (Windsor: NFER-Nelson).

Davis, K. (1987) 'Pressed to Death', *Coalition News*, vol. 1, no. 4.

Davis, K. (1986) *Developing our own Definitions – Draft for Discussion* (London: British Council of Organisations of Disabled People).

Davis, K. (1990) 'Old medicine is still no cure', *Community Care*.

Davis, K. (1993) 'On the Movement' in Swain *et al.*

Davis, K. and Mullender, A. (1993) *Ten Turbulent Years* (Nottingham: Centre for Social Action, University of Nottingham).

De Jong, G. (1983) 'Defining and Implementing the Independent Living Concept', in Crewe, N. and Zola, I. (eds) *Independent Living for Physically Disabled People* (Jossey-Bass: London).

Dept of Health (1989) *Caring for People* (London: HMSO).

Despouy, L. (1991) *Human Rights and Disability* (New York: United Nations Economic and Social Council).

Dessent, T. (1987) *Making the Ordinary School Special* (London: Falmer).

Disability Alliance (1988) *The Financial Circumstances of Disabled Adults Living in Private Households: A Disability Alliance Briefing on the Second OPCS Report* (London: Disability Alliance).

Dohrenwend, B. P. and Dohrenwend, B. S. (1974) *Stressful Life Events: Their Nature and Effects.* (New York: John Wiley).

Doyal, L. and Gough, I. (1991) *A Theory of Human Needs* (Basingstoke Macmillan).

Doyle, N. and Harding, T. (1992) 'Community care: Applying procedural fairness' in Coote, A. (ed.) *The Welfare of Citizens* (London: Rivers Oram).

Drake, R. (1994) 'The exclusion of disabled people from positions of power in British Voluntary Organisations', *Disability and Society*, vol. 9, No. 4.

Driedger, D. (1988) *The Last Civil Rights Movement* (London: Hurst & Co).

ENIL (1989) Press Release 'European Network on Independent Living'.

Ellis, K. (1993) *Squaring the Circle* (York: Joseph Rowntree Foundation).

Engels, F. (1844) *The Condition of the English Labouring Classes* (London: Panther).

Estes, C. (1984) in *Readings in the Political Economy of Ageing*, Swan, J. and Gerard, L. (eds) (New York: Baywood).

Estes, C., Swan, J. and Gerard, L., (1982) 'Dominant and Competing Paradigms in Gerontology: Towards a Political Economy of Ageing' *Ageing and Society*, vol. 2, no. 2.

Fenton, M. (1989) *Passivity to Empowerment* (London: RADAR).

Finkelstein, V. (1980) *Attitudes and Disabled People: Issues for Discussion* (New York: World Rehabilitation Fund).

Finkelstein, V. (1988) 'Changes in thinking about disability', unpublished paper.

Finkelstein, V. (1994) personal communication.

Finkelstein, V. (1993) 'Disability: a social challenge or an administrative responsibility' in Swain *et al.*

The Fish Report (1985) *Educational Opportunities for All?* (London: ILEA).

Flacks, D. (1991) 'Making History and Making Theory: Notes on How Intellectuals Seek Relevance' in Lemert (1991).

Ford, J., Mongon, D. and Whelan, E. (1982) *Special Education and Social Control* (London: Routledge & Kegan Paul).

Foucault, M. (1972) *The Archaeology of Knowledge* (New York: Pantheon).

Foucault, M. (1991) *Remarks on Marx* (New York: Semiotext(e)).

Freeden, M. (1991) *Rights* (Milton Keynes: Open University Press).

Freidson, E. (1970) *Profession of Medicine: a study in the sociology of applied knowledge* (New York: Dodd, Mead and Co.).

Freire, P. (1972) *Pedagogy of the Oppressed* (New York: Seabury).

French, S. (1993) 'Disability, impairment or something inbetween?' in Swain *et al.*

Fry, E. (1986) *An Equal Chance for Disabled People: A Study of Discrimination in Employment* (London: Spastics Society).

Fulcher, G. (1989) 'Integrate or Mainstream' in Barton, L. (1989, b).

Gillespie-Sells, K. (1993) 'Sing if you're happy that way', *Rights Not Charity*, vol. 1, no. 2.

Gillespie-Sells, K. (1994) 'Getting things right', *Community Care Inside* 31 March.

Goacher, B., Evans, J., Welton, J. and Wedell, K. 91988) *Policy and Provision for Special Educational Needs: Implementing the 1981 Act* (London: Cassell).

Goodall, L. (1988) 'Living Options for Physically Disabled People', *Disability, Handicap and Society*, 3, 2.

Gouldner, A. (1975) *For Sociology: Renewal and Critique in Sociology Today* (Harmondsworth: Pelican Books).

Gregory, J. (1987) *Sex, Race and the Law* (London: Sage).

Groce, N. (1985) *Everyone Here Spoke Sign Language: Hereditary Deafness on Martha's Vineyard* (London: Harvard University Press).

HMSO (1989) *Caring for People* (London: HMSO).

HMSO (1990) *Encouraging Citizenship* (London: HMSO).

Hall, S. (1979) 'The Great Moving Right Show', Cobden Trust Annual Lecture.

Hanks, J. and Hanks, L. (1980) 'The Physically Handicapped in Certain Non-Occidental Societies' in Phillips, W. and Rotenberg, J. (eds) *Social Scientists and the Physically Handicapped* (London: Arno Press).

Harris, C. (1983) 'Associational participation in old age' in Jerrome, D. (ed.) *Ageing in Modern Society* (London: Croom Helm).

Harrison, J. (1987) 'Severe Physical Disability: Responses to the Challenge of Care' (Cassell: London).

Hasler, F. (1993) 'Developments in the Disabled People's Movement' in Swain *et al.*

Havighurst, R., Neugarten, B. and Sheldon, S. (1968) 'Disengagement and patterns of ageing' in: Neugarten, B. (ed.) *Middle Age and Ageing: A Reader in Social Psychology* (Chicago: University of Chicago Press).

Hearn, K. (1991) 'Disabled Lesbians and Gays Are Here to Stay' in Kaufman, T. and Lincoln, P. (eds) *High Risk Lives: Lesbian and Gay Politics After the Clause* (Bridport: Prism Press).

Hegarty, S. and Pocklington, K. (1982) *Integration in Action* (Windsor: NFER-Nelson).

Hevey, D. (1991) 'Review of The Politics of Disablement' *DIAL* 22–1–91.

Hevey, D. (1992) *The Creatures Time Forgot: Photography and Disability Imagery* (London: Routledge).

Hewitt, M. (1993) 'Social movements and social need: problems with postmodern political theory', *Critical Social Policy*, Issue 37 52–74.

Higgins, P. (1985) *The Rehabilitation Detectives: doing human service work* (London: Sage).

Hill, M. (1992) 'Conference Address' *in Race and Disability: A dia-

*logue for action* (London: Greater London Association of Disabled People).

Hill, M. (1994) 'Getting things right', *Community Care Inside*, 31 March.

Holden, G. (1990) 'RADAR's New Director; Bert Massie Talks to Geraldine Holden', *Disability Now*, April.

Holdsworth, A. (1993) 'Our Allies Within', *Coalition*, July 1993.

Hoyes, L., Jeffers, S., Lart, R., Means, R. and Taylor, M. *User Empowerment and the Reform of Community Care* (Bristol: School for Advanced Urban Studies).

Hugman, R. (1991) *Power and the Caring Professions* (Basingstoke: Macmillan).

Humphrey, R. (1994) 'Thoughts on Disability Arts', *DAM*, vol. 4, no. 1.

Humphreys, S. and Gordon, P. (1992) *Out of Sight: The Experience of Disability 1900–1950* (Plymouth: Northcote House Publishers).

Hunter, D. (ed.) (1988) *Bridging the Gap: Case Management and Advocacy for People with Physical Handicaps* (London: King's Fund).

Hutchinson, D. and Tennyson, C. (1986) *Transition to Adulthood* (London: Further Education Unit).

Ignatieff, M. (1989) 'Citizenship and Moral Narcissism', *Political Quarterly*.

Illich, I. (1975) *Medical Nemesis: The Expropriation of Health* (London: Marion Boyers).

Jones, N. and Southgate, T. *The Management of Special Needs in Ordinary Schools* (London: Routledge).

Keeble, U. (1979) *Aids and Adaptations* (London: Bedford Square Press).

Keep, J. and Clarkson, J. (1993) *Disabled People have Rights* (London: RADAR).

Keith, L. (ed.) (1994) *Mustn't Grumble* (London: The Women's Press).

Kestenbaum, A. (1992) *Cash for Care: a report on the experience of Independent Living Fund clients* (Independent Living Fund).

Kittrie, N. (1971) *The Right to be Different: deviance and enforced therapy* (Baltimore: Johns Hopkins Press).

Knight, R. and Warren, M. (1978) *Physically Handicapped People Living at Home: A Study of Numbers and Needs* (London: HMSO).

Kuhn, T. (1961) *The Structure of Scientific Revolutions* (Chicago: University Press).

Lakey, J. (1993) *Paying for Independence* (London: Policy Studies Institute).

Lather, P. (1987), 'Research as Praxis', *Harvard Educational Review*, vol. 6, no. 3.

Lenin, V. I. (1902) 'What is to be done', *Collected Works*, vol. 5 (Moscow: Foreign Languages Publishing House, 1961).

Lemert, C. (1991) *Intellectuals and Politics: Social Theory in a Changing World* (London: Sage).

Lister, R. (1991) *The Exclusive Society: Citizenship and the Poor* (London: CPAG).

Lonsdale, S. (1986) *Work and Inequality* (London: Longman).

Lukes, S. (1974) *Power: a radical view* (London, Macmillan).

Lukes, S. (1974) *Individualism* (Oxford: Basil Blackwell).

Lunt, N. and Thornton, P. (1994) 'Disability and employment: towards an understanding of discourse and policy', *Disability and Society*, vol. 9, no. 1, 223–38.

MIND (1990) *The Right to Vote* (Preston: MIND).

Manning, N. and Oliver, M. (1985) 'Madness, Epilepsy and Medicine' in Manning, N. (ed.) *Social Problems and Welfare Ideology* (Aldershot: Gower).

Marshall, T. H. (1952) *Citizenship and Social Class* (Cambridge University Press).

Martin, J., Meltzer, H. and Elliot, D. (1988) *OPCS Surveys of Disability in Great Britain: Report 1 – The prevalence of disability among adults* (London: HMSO).

Martin, J. and White, A. (1988) *OPCS Surveys of Disability in Great Britain: Report 2 – The financial circumstances of disabled adults living in private households* (London: HMSO).

Martin, J. and White, A. (1988) *The Financial Circumstances of Disabled Adults Living in Private Households* (London: OPCS).

Martin, J., White, A. and Meltzer, H. *Disabled Adults: Services, Transport and Employment* (London: OPCS).

Marx, K. (1913) *A Contribution to the Critique of Political Economy* (Chicago University Press).

Marx, K. and Engels, F. (1967) *The Communist Manifesto* (Harmondsworth: Penguin).

Mason, M. and Rieser, R. (1990) *Disability Equality in the Classroom: A Human Rights Issue* (London: ILEA).

Mechanic, D. (1962) *Students under Stress* (New York: Free Press).

Meltzer, H., Smyth, M. and Robus, N. (1989) *Disabled Children: Services, Transport and Education* (London: HMSO).

Merton, R. (1968) *Social Theory and Social Structure* (New York: Free Press).

Miles, M. (1989) 'Rehabilitation Development in South West Asia: Conflicts and Potentials' in Barton, L. (1939a).

Ming Guo (1993) 'Demographic Features of People with Disabilities in China', *Disability, Handicap and Society*, vol. 8, no. 207–10.

Moore, J, and Morrison, J. (1988) *Someone Else's Problem* (Sussex: Falmer Press).

Morris, J. (1989) *Able Lives: Women's Experience of Paralysis* (London: Women's Press).

Morris, J. (1991) *Pride against Prejudice* (London: Womens Press).

Morris, J. (1992) *Disabled Lives* (London: BBC Educational Publications).

Morris, J. (1992) 'Tyrannies of Perfection', *New Internationalist*, no. 293, July.

Morris, J. (1992) 'Personal and Political: A Feminist Perspective in Researching Physical Disability' *Disability, Handicap and Society*, vol. 7, no. 2.

Morris, J. (1993a) *Community Care or Independent Living?* (York: Joseph Rowntree Foundation).

Morris, J. (1993b) *Independent Lives?: Community Care and Disabled People* (Basingstoke: Macmillan).

Morrison, E. and Finkelstein, V. (1993) 'Culture as Struggle; Access to Power' in Swain *et al.*

Neugarten, B. and Hagestad, G. (1976) 'Age and the life course' in

Binstock, R. and Shanas, E. (eds) *Handbook of Ageing and the Social Sciences* (New York: Van Nostrand Reinhold).

NCC (1990) *Education for Citizenship* (York: National Curriculum Council).

Oliver, M. (1978) 'Medicine and Disability: Steps in the Wrong Direction', *International Journal of Medical Engineering and Technology*, vol. 2, no. 3.

Oliver, M. (1980) Epilepsy, Crime and Delinquency: A Sociological Account, *Sociology*, vol. 14, no. 3.

Oliver, M. (1981) 'Disability, Adjustment and Family Life', in Brechin, A., Liddiard, P. and Swain, J., *Handicap in a Social World* (London: Hodder & Stoughton).

Oliver, M. (1982) 'A New Model of the Social Work Role in Relation to Disability, in J. Campling (ed.) *The Handicapped Person: a new perspective for social workers?* (London: RADAR).

Oliver, M. (1983) *Social Work with Disabled People* (Basingstoke: Macmillan).

Oliver, M. (1985a) 'Discrimination, Disability and Social Policy' in *Yearbook of Social Policy* Jones and Brenton.

Oliver, M. (1985b) 'The Integration–Segregation Debate: Some Sociological Considerations', *British Journal of Sociology of Education*, vol. 6, no. 1.

Oliver, M. (Spring 1987) 'Re-defining Disability: Some Implications for Research', *Research, Policy and Planning*, no. 5.

Oliver, M. (1988) 'The Political Context of Educational Decision-making: the Case of Special Needs', in L. Barton (ed.) *The Politics of Special Needs* (Sussex: Falmer Press).

Oliver, M. (1989a) 'Conductive Education: If it wasn't so sad it would be funny', *Disability, Handicap and Society*, vol. 4, no. 2.

Oliver, M. (1989b) 'Disability and Dependency: A Creation of Industrial Societies', in Barton, L. (ed.) *Disability and Dependency* (Brighton: Falmer Press).

Oliver, M. (1989c) 'Social Work and the Social Model of Disability: Some Current Reflections' in *Social Work and the Social Welfare Yearbook*, ed. Carter, P., Jeffs, T., and Smith, M. (Milton Keynes: Open University Press).

Oliver, M. (1990) *The Politics of Disablement* (Basingstoke: Macmillan and St Martin's Press).

Oliver, M. (1991a) 'Disability and Participation in the Labour Market' in Brown, P. and Scase, R. (eds) *Poor Work* (Milton Keynes: Open University Press).

Oliver, M. (1991b) 'Reappraising Special Needs Education: A Review', *European Journal of Special Needs Education*, vol. 6, no. 1.

Oliver, M. (1992a) 'Changing the Social Relations of Research Production' *Disability, Handicap and Society*.

Oliver, M. (1992b) 'Intellectual Masturbation: A Response to Soder and Booth', *European Journal of Special Needs Education*, vol. 7, no. 1.

Oliver, M. (ed.) (1991) *Social Work: Disabled People and Disabling Environments* (London: Kingsley Press).

Oliver, M. and Barnes, C. (1991) 'Discrimination, Disability and Welfare: From Needs to Rights' in Bynoe *et al.*

Oliver, M. and Zarb, G. (1989) 'The Politics of Disability: A New Approach', *Disability, Handicap and Society*, vol. 4, no. 3.

Oliver, M. and Zarb, G. (1992) *Personal Assistance Schemes: An Evaluation* (London: Greenwich Association of Disabled People).

Oliver, M., Zarb, G., Silver, J., Moore, M., Salisbury, V. (1988) *Walking into Darkness: The Experience of Spinal Injury* (Basingstoke: Macmillan).

Pagel, M. (1988) *On Our Own Behalf; An Introduction to the Self-organisation of Disabled People* (Manchester: GMCDP Publications).

Papadakis, E. (1993) 'Interventions in New Social Movements' in Hammersley, M. (ed.) *Social Research: Philosophy, Politics and Practice* (London: Sage Publications).

Parker, G. (1993) *With This Body: Caring and Disability in Marriage* (Milton Keynes: Open University Press).

Parsons, T. (1951) *The Social System* (New York: Free Press).

Percy-Smith, J. and Sanderson, I. (1992) *Understanding Local Needs* (London: IPPR).

Pinet, G. (1990) *Is the Law Fair to the Disabled?* (Copenhagen: World Health Organisation Regional Office for Europe).

Phillipson, C. (1982) *Capitalism and the Construction of Old Age* (London: Macmillan).

Potts, P. (1989) 'Working Report: Educating Children and Young People with Disabilities or Difficulties in Learning in The People's Republic of China' in Barton, L. (1989b).

Rabinow, P. (ed.) (1984) *The Foucault Reader* (New York: Pantheon Books).

Ramasut, A. (1989) *Whole School Approaches to Special Needs* (Sussex: Falmer Press).

Reason, P. (ed.) (1988) *Human Inquiry in Action: Developments in New Paradigm Research* (London: Sage).

Reichard, S. (1968) *Ageing and Personality* (New York: Wiley).

Rieser, R. and Mason, M. (1990) *Disability Equality in the Classroom; A Human Rights Issue* (London: ILEA).

Rowan, J. (1981) 'A Dialectical Paradigm for Research, in Reason, P. and Rowan, J. (eds) *Human Inquiry: A Source Book of New Paradigm Research* (Chichester: John Wiley & Son).

Royal College of Physicians (1986) *Physical Disability in 1986 and Beyond* (London).

Ryan, J. and Thomas, F. (1980) *The Politics of Mental Handicap* (Harmondsworth: Penguin).

SSI (1991) *Care Management and Assessment – Managers' Guide* (London: HMSO).

Safilios-Rothschild, C. (1970) *The Sociology and Social Psychology of Disability and Rehabilitation* (New York: Random House).

Sayer, J. and Jones, N. (1987) *Teacher training and special educational needs* (London: Croom Helm).

Scotch, R. (1984) *From Goodwill to Civil Rights: Transforming Federal Disability Policy* (Philadelphia: Temple University Press).

Scott, A. (1990) *Ideology and New Social Movements* (London: Unwin Hyman).

Shakespeare, T. (1992) 'A Response to Liz Crow', *Coalition*, September 1992.

Shakespeare, T. (1993) 'Disabled People's Self-organisation: a new social movement?' *Disability, Handicap and Society*, vol. 8, no. 3, 249–64.

Shakespeare, T. (1993) 'Allies, Advocates and Obstacles', *Coalition*, October 1993.

Shanas, E., Townsend, P. and Wedderburn, D. *et al.* (1968) *Old People in Three Industrial Societies* (London: RKP).

Silver, R. and Wortman, C. (1980) 'Coping with Undesirable Life Events' in Gerber, J. and Seligman, M. (eds) *Helplessness Theory and Applications* (London: Academic Press).

Smith, S. (1989) *The Politics of Race and Residence* (Cambridge: Polity Press).

Spastics Society (1992) *Polls Apart: Disabled People and the 1992 General Election* (London: Spastics Society).

Spender, D. (1982) *Women of Ideas (and What Men have Done to Them)* (London: Ark).

Squires, P. (1990) *Anti-Social Policy: Welfare, Ideology and the Disciplinary State* (London: Harvester Wheatsheaf).

Stanton, I. (1991) 'Freewheelin', *Coalition*, April 1991, 20–23.

Stevens, A. (1993) 'Communicating with Users: Learning a User Led Perspective through Reflective Practice' in Stevens, A. (ed.) *Back from the Wellhouse: discussion papers on sensory impairment and training in community care* (London: CCETSW, Paper 32.1).

Stevenson, O. and Parsloe, P. (1993) *Community Care and Empowerment* (York: Joseph Rowntree Foundation).

Stone, D. (1985) *The Disabled State* (Basingstoke: Macmillan).

Strauss, A. and Glaser, B. (1967) *The Discovery of Grounded Theory* (Chicago: Aldine).

Strauss, A. and Glaser, B. (1975) *Status Passage* (Chicago: Aldine).

Stuart, O. (1992) 'Race and Disability: What Type of Double Disadvantage' *Disability, Handicap and Society*, vol. 7, no. 2.

Sutherland, A. (1981) *Disabled We Stand* (London: Souvenir Press).

Swain, J. (1992) Personal communication by letter.

Swain, J. (1993) 'Taught Helplessness? Or a say for disabled students in schools' in Swaim *et al.* (1993).

Swain, J., Finkelstein, V. French, S. and Oliver, M. (1993) *Disabling Barriers – Enabling Environments* (London: Sage).

Swann, W. (1990) *Integration Statistics* (London: CSIE).

Swann, W. (1991) *Integration Statistics: LEAs Reveal Local Variations 1982–7* (Bristol: Centre for Studies on Inclusive Education).

Swann, W. (1992) *Integration Statistics: English LEAs 1988–91* (Bristol: Centre for Studies on Inclusive Education).

Taylor, D. (1989) 'Citizenship and Social Power', *Critical Social Policy*, no. 26.

Taylor, G. and Bishop, J. (eds) (1991) *Being Deaf: The Experience of Deafness* (London: Pinter Publishers).

Thomson, P. (1993) *Cause for Concern: What Directors of Social Services think about the Impact of the Changes to the Independent Living Fund* (London: DIG).

Thompson, P., Lavery, M. and Curtice, J. (1990) *Shortchanged by Disability* (London: Disablement Income Group).

Tomlinson, S. (1981) *A Sociology of Special Education* (London: Routledge & Kegan Paul).

Tomlinson, S. (1982) *A Sociology of Special Education* (London: Routledge and Kegan Paul).

Topliss, E. and Gould, B. (1981) *A Charter for the Disabled* (Oxford: Blackwell).

Topliss, E. (1983) *Social Responses to Handicap* (London: Longman).

Touraine, A. (1981) *The Voice and the Eye: An Analysis of Social Movements* (Cambridge: Cambridge University Press).

Turner, B. (1984) *The Body and Society* (Oxford: Basil Blackwell).

Turner, B. (1986) *Citizenship and Capitalism* (London: Allen & Unwin).

UPIAS (1976) *Fundamental Principles of Disability* (London: Union of the Physically Impaired Against Segregation).

United Nations (1975) *Declaration on the Rights of Disabled Persons.*

Vasey, S. (1992) 'A Response to Liz Crow', *Coalition*, September 1992.

Walker, A. (1980) 'The Social Creation of Poverty and Dependency in Old Age', *Journal of Social Policy*, vol. 9 (1): 45–75.

Wallach Balogh, R. (1991) 'Learning from Feminism: Social Theory and Intellectual Vitality' in Lemert, C. (ed.) *Intellectuals and Politics: Social Theory in a Changing World* (London: Sage Publications).

Walmsley, J. (1991) 'Talking to Top People: some issues relating to the citizenship of people with learning difficulties', *Disability, Handicap and Society*, vol. 6, no. 1.

Walton, J. (1979) 'Urban Political Economy', *Comparative Urban Research.*

Ward, L. (1987) *Talking Points: the Right to Vote* (London: CMH).

Wardhaugh, J. and Wilding, P. (1993) 'Towards an explanation of the corruption of care', *Critical Social Policy*, no. 37.

Warnock Report (1978) *Report of the Committee of Enquiry into the Education of Handicapped Children and Young People* (London: HMSO).

West, J. (ed.) (1992) *The Millbank Quarterly Supplements 1/2 – The Americans with Disabilities Act: From Policy to Practice* (Cambridge University Press).

Williams, F. (1989) *Social Policy: A Critical Introduction* (Cambridge Polity Press).

Williams, G. H. (1983) 'The Movement for Independent Living: An Evaluation and Critique', *Social Science and Medicine*, 17, 15.

Williams, G. H. (1991) 'Disablement and the Ideological Crisis in Health Care', *Social Science and Medicine*, vol. 33, no. 4, pp. 517–24.

Wolfensberger, W. (1989) 'Human service policies: The rhetoric versus the reality' in Barton, L. (ed.) *Disability and Dependency*, (London: Falmer Press).

Wood, P. (1980) *International Classification of Impairments, Disabilities and Handicaps* (Geneva: World Health Organisation).

Zarb, G. (1992) 'On the Road to Damascus: First steps towards changing the Relations of Research Production', *Disability, Handicap and Society* vol. 7, no. 2.

Zarb, G, and Oliver, M. (1993) *Ageing with a Disability: What do they expect after all these years?* (London: University of Greenwich).

# Index

Printed in the United States
85858LV00002B/103/A